Fredericksburg
History & Biography

Volume 15, 2016

Central Virginia
Battlefields Trust

Central Virginia Battlefields Trust, Inc.
Fredericksburg, Virginia

CENTRAL VIRGINIA BATTLEFIELDS TRUST

Board of Directors
Harriett M. Condon
Edward J. Geller
Bradley M. Gottfried
J. Michael Greenfield
Lloyd B. Harrison, III
Robert Lee Hodge
Peter R. Kolakowski
Robert K. Krick
Charles G. McDaniel
James M. Pates
Eric Powell
Thomas A. Van Winkle
Linda P. Wandres

Executive Director
Ben Brockenbrough

President
Thomas A. Van Winkle

Vice President
Harriett M. Condon

Secretary
Robert K. Krick

Treasurer
Lloyd B. Harrison, III

Editor
Erik F. Nelson

Table of Contents

V   Introductory Notes

9   Never Forgotten: Sergeant Jerome Peirce of the 36th Massachusetts Infantry Regiment
By Josef W. Rokus

31   At Spottsylvania: Mr. Beadle at the Scene of a Bloody Battle
An 1895 article annotated by Erik F. Nelson

41   Minutes of the Common Council of the Town of Fredericksburg, 1868-1869
Typescript corrected and annotated by Erik F. Nelson

103   A Murder in Fredericksburg
By Elizabeth Parnicza

119   Southern Exposure
By Noel G. Harrison and Erik Nelson

125   Index

Property Acquired by the Central Virginia Battlefields Trust

The CVBT has helped to preserve historic terrain at four major battlefields. Over 1,000 acres of critical ground that would otherwise have been lost to development have been acquired in fee simple (sometimes in partnership with other organizations) or have been placed under an easement. The breakdown, by battlefield, is as follows:

FREDERICKSBURG
Willis Hill
Pelham's Corner
Latimer's Knoll
Braehead
Slaughter Pen Farm

CHANCELLORSVILLE
McLaw's Wedge
Nine Mile Run
Talley Farm
Orange Plank Road
Smith Run
May 1 Field
Flank Attack

WILDERNESS
Grant's Knoll
Wilderness Crossroads

SPOTSYLVANIA COURT HOUSE
Po River/Block House Bridge
Harris Farm

Introductory Notes

The Central Virginia Battlefields Trust has been incorporated for twenty years. During those two decades, it has helped to preserve more than 1,000 acres of historic terrain in and around Fredericksburg, Virginia. We did not begin publishing this journal until a few years after our inception, but we thought it important to develop a scholarly basis for our land acquisition efforts. This volume is the fifteenth in the resulting series and we are proud to be able to share the historic context within which we preserve dirt and grass.

As we have presented since Volume 1 was published, in 2002, the land we preserve had a history before the war and its disposition after the war has also varied. Some land was acquired for preservation, to keep it as it looked in the nineteenth century. Other land is of interest, but will never be preserved because it has been developed by a growing community. Over the years, this journal has looked into all aspects of the Fredericksburg area's historic landscape and this volume is no exception. The following authors have generously contributed their research to this journal and most of them are likely familiar to many of our readers:

Josef W. Rokus received a B.S. and an M.S. from the University of Illinois as well as an M.B.A. from Dartmouth College. He is an Army veteran who served with a signals battalion in Southeast Asia and has written a book about his unit called *The Professionals: History of the Phu Lam, Vietnam U.S. Army Communications Base*. Joe is an excellent (thorough) researcher and has written several articles that relate to local Fredericksburg history. In this volume he shares the story of a Union soldier named Jerome Peirce who is buried in the Fredericksburg National Cemetery. The remains of fallen men in the rough and tangled woodlands around Fredericksburg area were not usually able to be identified when they were recovered years after the battles had been fought. As a consequence, the cemetery has huge numbers of graves marked unknown. Jerome Peirce, however, is not only identified, but his grave is decorated with flowers every Memorial Day. He has no direct descendants, but somebody has remembered him every year for more than a century.

Erik F. Nelson is a Navy veteran and a graduate of the University of California, Santa Barbara, where he earned a Bachelors and a Masters in History. He was an ordnance specialist, which drew him to an 1895 article about the Spotsylvania Court House battlefield, which includes a short but tragic story of a young boy killed by an exploding shell long after the battle had ended. He is the Senior Planner for the City of Fredericksburg as well as the City Archivist, which has brought him in contact with the old City Council files. This journal has been presenting the Fredericksburg Town Council minutes in two year increments, beginning in the Civil War years and continuing through Reconstruction. This volume includes the period 1868-1869. Those were the years when the town government found itself under martial law, its mayor appointed by an outside authority, which was something that had never occurred during the war itself.

Elizabeth Parnicza is a 2011 graduate of West Virginia University. After earning a Bachelor's degree in History, she moved to the "other" Virginia to pursue her passion for the Civil War. She serves as a park historian at the Fredericksburg and Spotsylvania National Military Park, where she supervises the Chancellorsville Battlefield Visitor Center and helps to coordinate the park's digital media. Beth's ongoing research is to examine how American society and the individual soldiers coped with the immense loss and change brought by the Civil War. In this volume, she delves into the murder of a Fredericksburg civilian by Federal soldiers who were stragglers from their units. The resulting court martial is of interest because the key witness was an African American. The testimony of a black individual would become unwelcome as the era of Jim Crow descended on the South, but for a brief period after the Civil War, the promise of equality under the law appeared to be within reach.

Noel G. Harrison is an historian with the Fredericksburg and Spotsylvania National Military Park, where he has served off and on for 30 years. He currently works in land-management and easements, but is also the author of two books on the Civil War in the Fredericksburg area, one book on a Spanish-American War camp in Fairfax County, several articles in this journal, and an illustrated guide to Civil War sites on the central grounds of the University of Mary Washington. He holds an M.A. in History from the University of Virginia. Noel is constantly searching for primary material and often finds archival gold, which he also generously shares. The photos he found for the Southern Exposure section are remarkably similar to the modern views, showing how well the National Park Service has been able to preserve that significant area. What should be noted, however, is that Sunken Road remained in public use as a roadway until well into the twenty-first century. The U.S. government owned the land, but the City of Fredericksburg owned the right of access, which it only relinquished when an alternate route became available to handle modern traffic. The Park has since restored the scene to its wartime appearance.

Erik F. Nelson
Editor

Jerome Peirce. Photo courtesy of the Patricia Mason family.

NEVER FORGOTTEN:
Sergeant Jerome Peirce of the 36th Massachusetts Infantry Regiment

By Josef W. Rokus

FLOWERS

On Memorial Day in 1993, the Fredericksburg *Free Lance-Star* featured an article titled "A lasting promise: Fallen Civil War soldier hasn't been forgotten." The story included a picture of Fredericksburg resident Lucille Heflin Ingalls and her grandson Kent Ingalls placing flowers at one of the many gravestones in the Fredericksburg National Cemetery. The lead sentence read: "The graveyard flowers had remained a mystery through the years."[1]

A few days earlier, Kent's fifth grade class at a Catholic grade school, close to the National Cemetery, was looking forward to the traditional Memorial Day honor of placing small American flags on all the graves. His teacher, Mary Ann Martin, was getting her class pepped up for the mammoth job and told her class the story of the flowers that mysteriously appear each Memorial Day at the gravestone of Corporal Jerome Pierce, a Union soldier from Massachusetts.

Kent realized his teacher was talking about something his family had always taken for granted. He told his classmates that some years after the Civil War the Pierce family had sent $100 to his great-great-great-grandfather, Andrew Birdsall, who was the superintendent of the Fredericksburg National Cemetery at the time. He was asked to deposit it into a bank account and use the interest to place flowers at Pierce's grave every Memorial Day. For well over a century, the Birdsall descendants had carried on the tradition, or maybe more appropriately, had accepted the duty to remember Pierce once a year.[2]

Andrew J. Birdsall. On the back of the original is the date 8/24/83. Photo obtained from Myers/Cook Family Tree, on Ancestry.com.

The *Free Lance-Star* reporter had contacted the Fredericksburg and Spotsylvania National Military Park, which administers the National Cemetery, but found that the records contained very little information about Pierce. The National Park Service staff knew he had enlisted in the 36th Massachusetts Infantry Regiment in 1862, at the age of 31, and that he had been killed on May 12, 1864, at the Bloody Angle, at Spotsylvania Court House. They knew nothing else about him. Andrew Birdsall's granddaughter, Alice Heflin Abernathy, had until recently taken on the responsibility for placing the flowers. About ten years earlier, Mrs. Abernathy had tried to put together the pieces of the puzzle and made some inquiries about Jerome Pierce's relatives in Massachusetts, but to no avail. In the newspaper article, she was quoted as saying: "The Birdsall side of the story would dearly love to meet the Pierce side, at least to let them know that their young corporal is remembered every Memorial Day." When several newspapers picked up the *Free Lance-Star* article from the Associated Press, the Jerome Pierce story spread beyond Fredericksburg.[3]

Henry Hurt, an editor for *Reader's Digest*, happened to see the *Free Lance-Star* story in his local newspaper and decided that if he could unearth more details about Pierce and his family, it could make an excellent article for his magazine. With the help of a professional researcher at the New England Historic Genealogical Society, Hurt gathered a wealth of data about Pierce before he enlisted, about his widow Albinia Jaquith Pierce, and their young daughter Lucy. He also found a distant Jaquith relative in Billerica, Massachusetts, who was able to locate the gravestone that marks the family plot in a local cemetery. The gravestone made clear that the correct spelling of Jerome's surname was "Peirce" instead of "Pierce," as it had been spelled on his gravestone in the Fredericksburg National Cemetery.[4]

The *Reader's Digest* research also turned up a treasure trove of letters that Corporal Peirce had written home during the war. They were held by Patricia Mason, of Dayton, Ohio, who was the great-grandniece of Albinia

Peirce. Hurt visited Ms. Mason in early 1994, where he found over 150 letters along with a number of Peirce family photographs. She had inherited the letters and photographs from her brother, who had been killed in Vietnam, and they had been squirreled away in an old box in the garage, with Ms. Mason not really knowing who Jerome Peirce had been.[5]

Jerome Peirce's Story

Jerome Peirce was born on November 11, 1830, in Niagara, New York. He was one of twelve children, but no information has been found about his early years or his education. At some point, his parents, Joseph and Martha Sherwin Peirce, moved the family to Billerica, Massachusetts. Peirce married Albinia Jaquith in the Congregational Church in Billerica on September 10, 1857.[6]

Albinia J. Peirce. Photo courtesy of the Patricia Mason family.

Jerome and Albinia had two children. Charles Jerome Peirce was born on July 10, 1858, but he died the same day. Their daughter, Lucy, was born on December 26, 1859, in Charlestown, Massachusetts. Apparently soon thereafter, the Peirce family relocated to Orange, Massachusetts, where he and his brother Joseph operated a small furniture manufacturing business. Various censuses and other records list his profession as chair maker, mechanic, engineer, and gilder. The 1860 U.S. Census lists Jerome, age 29, Albinia, age 25, and Lucy, age 6 months. The Civil War broke out the next year.[7]

Peirce did not rush to enlist at the start of the war, but he did respond to President Abraham Lincoln's July 2, 1862 call for 300,000 volunteers to serve for three years. He enlisted on August 4, 1862, with the rank of corporal. Fourteen men from Orange also signed up on that date, with seven more over the next four days. Since the population of the Town of Orange as of the 1860 Census was only 1,622, Peirce probably knew most, if not all, of the young men who volunteered with him. Their ages ranged from 18 to 39, with Peirce being 31 years old at the time.[8]

Why did Jerome Peirce join the Union army at an age several years older than most enlistees and leave a wife and young daughter behind? The Reverend Levi Ballou's sermon at Peirce's funeral service on June 19, 1864, provides some insight:

> *By frequent intercourse with him, I learned something of the struggle that was then going on in his mind in regard to the perilous condition of our beloved country. Long before he volunteered his services, he frequently spoke of the great wickedness of the present Rebellion as a crime utterly unjustifiable in the sight of God or men and of the duty of sustaining and upholding the government.... In his view, there were evidently but two courses to pursue in the present crisis of our national affairs, either, nobly to defend and sustain the government at whatever cost it may be, or shrinking from duty, leave it to be dismembered and perish, and thus bring upon ourselves the reproach and scorn of the civilized world. There was no middle ground to be taken.*[9]

After the newly formed regiments had been assembled in Worcester, Massachusetts, the volunteers were officially mustered into Federal service on August 27, 1862. Corporal Peirce was assigned to Company H of the 36th Massachusetts Infantry Regiment. With minimal training, the regiment left for Boston and from there went to Alexandria, Virginia, and on to Washington, D.C. Assigned to Major General Ambrose Burnside's Ninth Corps, the regiment soon found itself in Maryland, but narrowly missed being engaged at Antietam. From there it moved into Virginia, ending up in Falmouth, across the Rappahannock River from Fredericksburg. At the December 1862 Battle of Fredericksburg, the 36th Massachusetts Regiment found itself held in reserve, below the town and across Hazel Run, in the area of the lower pontoon crossing. In January 1863, the regiment participated in the disastrous "Mud March." When Burnside was relieved as commander of the Army of the Potomac, he and his Ninth Corps were reassigned to the Western Theater.[10]

From March 1863 until early April 1864, the men of the 36th Massachusetts crisscrossed Kentucky, participated in a portion of the Vicksburg campaign, moved to Jackson, Mississippi, returned to Kentucky, and then marched into eastern Tennessee. They took part in a battle at Campbell's Station and in late 1863, supported the defense of Knoxville. The regiment then spent more time in eastern Tennessee before being ordered to Annapolis, Maryland, where it arrived on April 6, 1864.[11]

After a few weeks in Annapolis, the regiment marched to Washington, D.C., where, President Lincoln and General Burnside reviewed the Ninth Corps to the cheers and well-wishes of a large crowd. In a letter to Albinia,

Peirce wrote: "A great day yesterday. We were received very enthusiastically by Genl. Burnside and President Lincoln on the balcony of the Willard Hotel to salute us as we passed. The boys got a 'pass' and remained in Washington last night. Had a good sight of Washington City. The president looks pale and careworn—very."[12]

For a short time in the fall of 1863, Peirce had been assigned to a special detail to return to Massachusetts for recruiting duty. Whether he was able to see his family has not been determined, but it is highly likely that he did. If so, it would have been the last time he saw his wife and young daughter. On January 1, 1864, he also received a promotion to sergeant, giving him a significant pay increase—from $13.00 as a corporal to $17.00 per month.

Although they had expected to be deployed on a coastal expedition, the Ninth Corps was instead assigned to guard the Orange and Alexandria Railroad, from Fairfax to the Rappahannock River. In late April, the 36th Massachusetts found itself scattered along the railroad line, as the Army of the Potomac concentrated near the Rapidan River, in preparation for its next campaign.

On May 4, 1864, the Army of the Potomac struck its tents and moved to cross the Rapidan River. The 36th Massachusetts crossed the pontoon bridges at Germanna Ford at daylight on May 5. The next day, the regiment proceeded to Wilderness Tavern, where it was ordered to prepare for action. On that second day of fighting in the Wilderness, the Ninth Corps entered the battle. By nightfall, the heavy fighting came to a halt and there were 85 fewer men of the 36th Massachusetts present for duty.[13]

On May 7, when the Federals started their advance toward Spotsylvania Court House, the 36th Massachusetts first moved back to Wilderness Tavern, where the Ninth Corps was being massed. The following morning, the regiment moved towards Chancellorsville, where it bivouacked and remained until about noon of May 9, when orders were received to move in the direction of Spotsylvania Court House. The Ninth Corps reached that new battlefield on May 11.[14]

Early on the morning of May 12, a cold and dismal day, the regiment advanced against an entrenched enemy line and drew first fire from the Confederate skirmishers at 4:30 a.m.. Several weeks later, Lieutenant Philip Woodward, who commanded Peirce's company, wrote a letter to Jerome Peirce's wife, now a widow, describing his sergeant's death and burial on the battlefield. As indicated in this transcription, a few of the words are not readable.

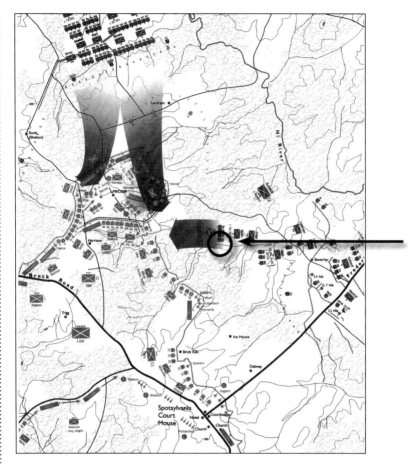

Sergeant Peirce was killed during an attack against the Confederate position at Spotsylvania Court House on May 12, 1864. The circle and the arrow indicate the position of his regiment, the 36th Massachusetts Infantry.

Near Petersburg, Va., July 4, 1864
Mrs. Jerome Peirce
Respecting Sergeant's death, I am afraid I can tell you but little more than J.H. has already written. I can with truth say that Sergt. was an esteemed friend of mine. That Co. H. had no other such a man—purely patriotic—philanthropic, ever lending a helping hand in sickness and working for his Comrades as well as for himself. His morals to the Lord [???] as you must know were strictly pure. No Profanity or Obscenities ever crossed his lips. [???] and while a soldier [???] he bore while at home. No one can say too much in

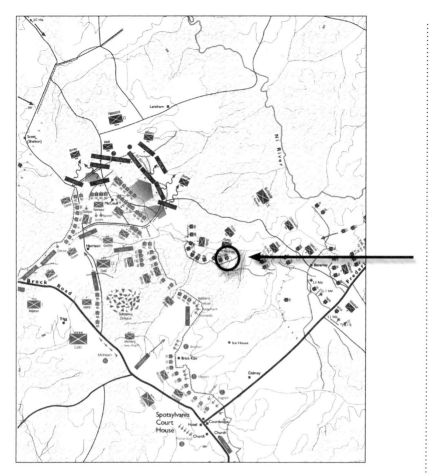

When the attacking Federals pulled back and entrenched, Sergeant Peirce's body lay between the lines. When darkness fell on May 12, 1864, his exhausted comrades took the time to recover and bury him. The circle and the arrow show his unit's location after its morning attack that day.

his Praise. His loss is felt not only in his family but in his Co. and Regt. and wherever he was known.

The two last nights that he lived Jerome and I slept together. On the morning of the 12th of May [we] went forth to meet the Enemy. Jerome knew our Danger yet faced it like a brave soldier and was first of our company to fall. I did not see him fall as we were falling back under a cover of a Fence, the enemy coming down on us and occupying the ground on which he fell. Consequently his body was in the Enemy's hands for about 15 minutes. When we charged forward we not only took the ground we lost but a great deal more. Jerome's body lay in a very exposed position [and] it was impossible to move it. But I went to him and took his Memorandum Book for I felt as though I ought to make an effort to secure some memento. The Book I gave to J.H. His body had to remain until after dark when we buried it the best that circumstances would permit. He was killed at about 7 o.c. [o'clock] AM. His other effects I turned over to J.H. I also found the Bullet that killed him. I took it from his left Breast—no one [???] after he was hit, he must have died instantly. His grave is in a Pine Grove—well marked.

I sympathize with you in your affliction and shall be happy to serve you when opportunity arises. If it [???] would very much like a photograph of Jerome.

   I am yours in sympathy
   Philip G. Woodward
   First (Lt.) Commanding Co. H 36th M.
   [Massachusetts] V. [Volunteers][15]

The day before, on July 3, 1864, the regiment's commanding officer had written the following official notification of Sergeant Peirce's death:

This is to certify that Jerome Peirce, a Sergeant of Company H, Thirty-sixth Regiment of Massachusetts Volunteers Infantry, was killed on May 12, 1864, at Spottsylvania Court House, Virginia, during an engagement with the enemy and that he was in the performance of his duty at the time.
   J. B. Smith
   Captain, Commanding Regiment[16]

Both of the above letters were written almost two months after the fighting at Spotsylvania Court House, which shows how relentless the 1864 Overland Campaign had been. Not until the regiment had reached Petersburg was there time to catch up on these necessary administrative details.

Re-interment

As the guns fell silent at Spotsylvania Court House, the horrors of the brutal fighting became more evident. The proximity of the two armies and the incessant fighting had left the soldiers from both sides with little time to bury fallen comrades. Consequently, the ground remained littered with many dead Union and Confederate soldiers. When the Confederates abandoned their positions, Union forces briefly occupied the contested ground.

To make the position tolerable, the Federal soldiers threw the bodies of the dead into the trenches formerly occupied by their foes and kicked dirt from the adjacent parapet down to cover them.

Numerous accounts of the conditions on the battlefield have described the awful scene. Major David E. Cronin of the 1st New York Mounted Rifles described what he saw at the Bloody Angle months after the battle: "It was a field impossible to describe adequately, having been precipitately abandoned by both combatants. It presented an awful picture of the magnitude and ferocity of the war. In some places the remains of the dead of both armies lay in mingled heaps, partly covered with mounds of brushwood, placed there by local citizens to prevent the ravages of wild hogs. In many other places the rain had washed bare the shallow burial-trenches, disclosing hundreds of uniformed skeletons; but many bodies lay unsheltered, just as they had fallen." These conditions show how easily Jerome Peirce's remains could have been lost and become just another "Unknown."[17]

The first postwar effort to inter the Union dead took place a year after the fighting. The First United States Veteran Volunteer Regiment, a collection of officers and men who had reenlisted in the army after previous service in other regiments, arrived at the Spotsylvania Court House battlefield on June 19, 1865. The men found where the Army of the Potomac had hastily buried many of the dead immediately after the battle. They also saw that Joseph Sanford, a local resident, had taken care of many of the rest. Sanford owned the Spotsylvania Court House Hotel and was the village's most prominent citizen. In May 1865, he had met Major General William T. Sherman, whose army was then passing through the area en route to Washington D.C. Sherman arranged for Sanford to bury the remains of the Union soldiers that still littered the ground and the innkeeper had tackled the job with energy. By the time the First Regiment reached the battlefield a month later, having first buried bodies in the Wilderness, they found relatively few bodies unburied. The regiment's commanding officer intended to create a cemetery for these remains, but the summer heat rendered them so putrid that he bowed to necessity and ordered his men to bury the skeletons where they lay. They were to mark those that could still be identified with headboards, so that friends and family members could later find them. According to the commanding officer's later report, the regiment had buried the bones of 1,500 men in the Wilderness and Spotsylvania Court House, identifying as many as possible, but also having to mark many as unknown. That report does not specifically mention Sergeant Peirce's temporary grave.[18]

The work done by the men of the First Regiment remained intact for just one year. In 1866, the federal government decided to consolidate the graves of the Union soldiers from that area of Virginia into a National Cemetery in Fredericksburg. The War Department selected Marye's Heights as the site, and began construction in June. The work to collect the remains of Federal soldiers from the large number of sites where bodies were to be found had actually begun a month earlier, by a burial corps of U.S. soldiers stationed in Fredericksburg. The task was enormous though, and the government was soon paying former slaves, Irish immigrants, and Confederate veterans $15 a month, plus lodging and rations, to do the work.[19]

By the end of 1866, substantial progress had been made across the country toward burying the concentrations of dead soldiers in existing burial grounds and in developing new cemeteries. The Fredericksburg National Cemetery would eventually contain more than 15,000 burials, approximately 84 percent of them classified as "Unknown." Over the next two years, burial parties scoured the Fredericksburg region, bringing in wagonloads of human remains. It took until the fall of 1868 to finish the work of removing the dead from the battlefields and transferring them to the cemetery for re-interment. The cemetery, however, was not blocked out by state, unit, or battle. Instead, bodies were buried as they were brought to the cemetery, and no records were kept regarding when particular individual remains were re-interred or where they had been found. If there was any comfort that Sergeant Peirce's family would ever be able to take in his death, it was that his comrades had been able to bury him in a temporary grave, marking its location sufficiently well that his remains could be identified when they were transferred to Grave No. 540 in the Fredericksburg National Cemetery.[20]

It appears that Albinia received the sad news about her husband's death sometime in mid or late May of 1864. A commemorative service was held on June 19, 1864, in Orange, Massachusetts. Afterward, Albinia moved back to the Boston area, to live with her parents, Franklin and Lucy Jaquith, in Billerica, Massachusetts. At that time, Franklin Jaquith was a 70-year old farmer. The other members of the household were his wife Lucy, 63, and their children Franklin, Jr., 29; Abigail (Abbie), 34; Mary, 28; and Joseph, 26. Albinia's widow's pension would finally be approved on

September 6, 1865, and made retroactive to the date when Sergeant Peirce had been killed.[21]

Albinia and Lucy Peirce

Albinia would continue to live with her parents and later, her brother. Her daughter Lucy was drawn to education. After graduating from the local high school in 1876, Lucy Peirce attended Salem Normal School (now Salem State University) in Salem, Massachusetts, which prepared her to teach in high schools. Her teaching career over the next 36 years included positions in Princeton, Massachusetts, Howard Seminary in West Bridgewater, Massachusetts, Sanborn Seminary in Kingston, New Hampshire, and the Allen Boys' School in West Newton, Massachusetts. In addition, she taught at the Curry School of Expression (now Curry College), and was also an assistant at the Widener Library at Harvard College.

Lucy also attended Radcliffe College for one year in 1899–1900 as a "special student," taking English and history courses. She subsequently worked with Radcliffe College's placement office for several years. Her correspondence with that office provides some additional details about her life. For example, in a letter from February 1913 she wrote: "I find I shall be obliged to leave my position soon. Of course, my deafness, which drove me out of the classroom, is a handicap in other places, but I am very anxious to return to some line of work more in accordance with my taste and training than that in mercantile offices. I am looking up libraries, correspondence schools, research work, etc." Her deafness was apparently the reason that she left the teaching profession and eventually worked at the Widener Library. In 1916, she made another career change by joining the World Peace Foundation in Boston, Massachusetts, where she was employed until 1935. Its mission then, and still today, is "educating all people about the waste and destructiveness of war." It is now affiliated with The Fletcher School of Law and Diplomacy at Tufts University.[22]

At some point, Albinia tried to determine where her husband had been buried. A lengthy obituary for Andrew J. Birdsall, published in a Massachusetts newspaper, confirms that Albinia and Lucy Peirce visited Fredericksburg at one time to see their loved one's grave. Andrew Birdsall had been the superintendent of the Fredericksburg National Cemetery and assisted Albinia in finding Jerome Peirce's grave. He would continue to decorate her husband's grave in later years and when he moved away, his daughter continued that tradition. The Birdsall obituary reads, in part, as follows:

It will be remembered that for long weary months after Mr. Jerome Peirce was slain in battle that no knowledge of his place of burial could be obtained by his bereaved widow and child. After casting about in many ways without success, and her brother, Franklin Jaquith, quietly resorting to correspondence with superintendents of different National cemeteries, a most definite and satisfactory response was received from Major Birdsall of Fredericksburg, stating reliable facts of his burial there.

His kindness was unlimited, his statements minute, photographic views were sent by him, and every memorial day he carefully accepted commissions for the floral decorations of the grave. And later, when Mrs. Peirce and her daughter visited the cemetery, Maj. Birdsall and family united in their hospitable attentions. After government removed his services to Hampton, his daughter has continued a kind interest in "the soldier's grave."[23]

Albinia Peirce died on February 29, 1920. Her daughter Lucy then lived in Newton, Massachusetts, and in the 1930 U.S. Census she was listed as 71 years old and employed as a "Filing clerk in a statistical office." Almost certainly that was the position she held with the World Peace Foundation. Lucy Peirce was counted for the last time by a U.S. census taker in 1940. She died on August 8, 1946, at age 86, which brought the story of Sergeant Jerome Peirce and his family to an end. There were no direct descendants, but a tradition of remembering him had been established in Fredericksburg.[24]

Accepting a Duty

Andrew J. Birdsall would be the recipient of $100 to commemorate Sergeant Jerome Peirce each Memorial Day, on behalf of his distant family. He had been born in Butternuts, New York, on July 10, 1837, and became a stonemason. On October 2, 1861, he enlisted as a corporal in Company E of the Second New York Heavy Artillery Regiment, at Staten Island, New York. That regiment saw active service in Virginia and Birdsall was wounded on August 14, 1864, at Second Deep Bottom. He was mustered out of the service on October 1, 1864.

On July 18, 1876, Andrew Birdsall was appointed to be a national cemetery superintendent, and he first served in that capacity at Baton Rouge and then at Chalmette, both cemeteries in Louisiana. He qualified for this position as a wounded veteran. In late November of 1883 Birdsall was transferred to the Fredericksburg National Cemetery, where he remained for nine years. In 1892, when he was transferred to Hampton National Cemetery, the Fredericksburg *Free Lance* reported: "Major A. J. Birdsall made many friends during his residence here, and a general regret is felt because of the change. Fredericksburg has so far been fortunate in the selection of the Superintendents of the beautiful Cemetery. They have been gentlemen who have easily assimilated with the people, and between them quickly grew a feeling of kindness and attachment. Major B. is no exception." It should be noted that Birdsall never held the rank of major. Instead, it was an honorary title given to him by the local residents.[25]

Andrew Birdsall died in Hampton, Virginia, on February 20, 1897, after a long illness. His body was brought back to Fredericksburg, where two of his daughters resided at the time. He was buried in Grave No. 6629 in the Fredericksburg National Cemetery, with Masonic honors. Birdsall's wife, Julia A. Birdsall, followed him to the grave on August 9, 1918, and was buried beside him in Grave No. 6668. She was survived by four married daughters, who would continue decorating Sergeant Peirce's grave each Memorial Day, as their father had done.[26]

Birdsall's diary provides some details on how Peirce's grave came to be decorated each Memorial Day. The diary entry for June 11, 1891, for instance, notes: "Mrs. Pierce also sent her thanks for what I had done for her husband's grave on Memorial Day. I got a picture taken of his grave."[27]

A small bankbook used by Birdsall's family, now held by the National Park Service, is identified as "Bankbook from The Farmers and Merchants State Bank of Fredericksburg, Virginia." The front cover carries the following hand-written note: "Pierce Birdsall Memorial Fund." The account is titled "IN ACCOUNT WITH Pierce-Birdsall Memorial Fund. Interest to use May 30th each year for flowers for graves." It should be noted that the account name reads "graves" instead of "grave." In addition to decorating Sergeant Peirce's grave, the family was also decorating those of Andrew and Julia Birdsall.[28]

The first entry in the bankbook is dated October 8, 1919, and it is a deposit of $100.00. This is followed by 104 additional entries, with the last one being on September 29, 1956, noting an interest deposit of $.79. There is a final notation: "Bal. transferred to new book 11/11/57." Over the 37 years that this bankbook was in use, the entries for interest ranged from $.50 to $2.25. The withdrawals are usually less than $6.00. Many of the withdrawals were

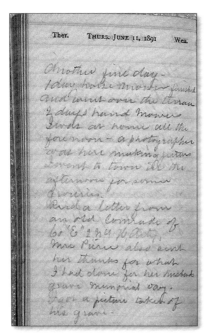

Superintendent Birdsall's diary. Original held in the collection of the Fredericksburg and Spotsylvania National Military Park.

made just prior to or around May 30th, but there is not a withdrawal every year, probably indicating that the Birdsall descendants also used flowers from their own gardens (as mentioned in one newspaper article). For the entire time this bankbook was used to track the Pierce-Birdsall Memorial Fund, the balance stayed close to $100, fluctuating from a low of $97.52 to a high of $110.65. The balance as of the last entry on September 29, 1956, was $102.84.[29]

Never Forgotten

The quiet tradition of decorating Sergeant Peirce's grave each Memorial Day went largely unnoticed until Kent Ingalls revealed to his grade school class that it was his family who had continued the task started by Andrew Birdsall. Following publication of that story, his daughter Alice Heflin Abernathy received a flurry of letters regarding the decoration of Peirce's grave. None of them were from anyone in Jerome Peirce's family or from the family of his widow, the Jaquiths, a well-established New England family, but these letters led to another front-page article in the *Free Lance-Star*, on December 27, 1993. The following are excerpts from that article:

The thought of a Southern lady solemnly decorating one Union soldier's grave every year must be powerfully poignant, because Fredericksburg's Alice Heflin Abernathy hasn't gotten this much mail since she closed her dress shop 20 years ago. Mrs. Abernathy, who will be 90 in February [1994] believes she's just doing her duty by keeping a promise her grandfather made to a Massachusetts family at least 120 years ago. She can't understand why people get so emotional about it, but she has certainly enjoyed getting letters from all over the country since her Memorial Day ritual was published in 1993.

The duty of decorating the grave has passed from Superintendent Birdsall down to Mrs. Abernathy, who fully expects her descendants to keep it up. I told myself, well Alice, you're the one who will do this. I was glad to do it. 'I even got so I'd call him Jerome,' she said. 'It didn't bother me a bit that he was a Yankee. I never thought about that.'

Letters began arriving at Mrs. Abernathy's house this summer [1993]. She is still getting them. Though they have tapered off to about one a week, most writers simply express admiration, such as the one from Ohio that said, "I have seldom been so moved by what someone does." Others provide clues about where Pierce's modern relatives might be. A letter that arrived the week of Thanksgiving had a short Pierce family tree and expressed sorrow that no living descendants could be found.[30]

When Mrs. Abernathy passed away at age 95 on August 31, 1999, her obituary noted she was the third generation caretaker of a Civil War soldier's grave in the Fredericksburg National Cemetery.[31]

On Memorial Day 1994, shortly after the *Reader's Digest* story appeared, another article in the Fredericksburg *Free Lance-Star* brought the story up-to-date. Although there are no direct Peirce descendants, there were descendants related to his wife, as the newspaper article reported:

Lt. Col. Peter Jaquith Casey of Billerica, Massachusetts, started reading about the solemn tradition in a recent Yankee Magazine article and realized that the story was about his family. Pierce's wife, Allie, was a Jaquith before she married. 'It's amazing, really,' Casey said. 'I had never thought about history or my family before.' Casey started poking around attics and basements, where he found letters about Allie Pierce's life. He visited a cemetery nearby and found a large marker for the Pierce family. It lists, among others, Allie, Jerome, and their daughter, Lucy, and mentions that Jerome is buried in Fredericksburg.[32]

The next time the Peirce story appeared in print was on May 24, 2001 and included the following:

[Alice Abernathy's niece] *Lucille Ingalls wouldn't think of letting Memorial Day pass unnoticed. She recalls Fredericksburg's Memorial Day parades of her childhood. 'The iris was always blooming, and we always picked flowers to put on the soldier's grave,' she said. 'It's been ingrained in us from the start.' Flowers are also placed on the graves of Birdsall and his wife, Julia, who are also buried in the National Cemetery. Others in the family often accompany Ingalls as well. She supposes the tradition will continue 'at least for another generation.'*

The words on the card accompanying the flowers have inspired those who pay their respects each Memorial Day: "Once lost, now found, never forgotten."[33]

J. Gary Ingalls, Kent's father, has since taken over the long-standing duty now passed down for several generations. Regarding his involvement, Gary Ingalls said, "At various times all three sisters and all cousins have participated. I went a few times as a child, but I became more involved in the 1990s when it became difficult for my mother to make the trip. By then it had become a real family tradition, and it was our family's way of honoring someone who died for the cause he deeply believed in, although my family knew very little about Jerome…. To the best of my knowledge, we have just paid for the grave decorations ourselves, and I really don't know the status of the account set up by my great-great-grandfather, Superintendent Andrew Birdsall. I know that before my mother passed away, she specifically and emphatically told me not to forget to decorate Jerome Peirce's grave every Memorial Day! I know that if for some reason I could not do it, my son, Kent, and one of my cousins would carry on the tradition."[34]

Correcting a Gravestone

The inscription on Sergeant Jerome Peirce's gravestone contains two errors. His rank at the time of his death was "Sergeant" instead of "Corporal" and the spelling of his surname should be "Peirce" instead of "Pierce." At the Fredericksburg National Cemetery, errors on gravestones have surfaced previously and the National Park Service's policy in the past was to correct information in the cemetery register, but to leave erroneous headstones in place. When descendants requested the correction of a stone, the park left the original headstone in place and placed a stone containing the proper information flat on the ground directly in front of it. This solution satisfied the descendants while maintaining the cemetery's historical integrity. There are at least seven graves in the Fredericksburg National Cemetery that have two gravestones.

Today, the National Park Service no longer permits second stones. Such additions to the historic landscape are thought to be inconsistent with their charge to maintain a designed historic landscape. The national cemeteries in the custody of the National Park Service deliberately retain the nineteenth century headstones and markers as they were installed, considering them as historic artifacts. This policy is unlike the approach taken by the Veterans Administration, which considers the soldier who is under the

In a cemetery where 85 percent of the remains are marked unknown, Sergeant Peirce has his own headstone. Unfortunately, both his name and rank are incorrect.

headstone. Any edits or corrections to information on the headstones is recorded and can be seen by the public in the Park's computerized database, but no physical changes are to be made until such time as the historic headstone requires replacement.[35]

The rationale behind the National Park Service's policy is certainly well-intended and perhaps even logical from the perspective of historic preservation. From the perspective of what a nation owes to someone who fought and died on its behalf, the policy prevents the correction of a young soldier's publicly visible headstone. Regardless of official considerations, Sergeant Jerome Peirce's grave continues to be decorated with flowers on Memorial Day.

∽ NOTES ∾

1. Amy Satterthwaite, "A lasting promise: Fallen Civil War soldier hasn't been forgotten," *Free Lance-Star* (Fredericksburg, Virginia), May 31, 1993.
2. Ibid. The article indicated that the Peirce family had sent Superintendent Birdsall $100 in the 1870s. Birdsall, however, was not appointed superintendent of the Fredericksburg National Cemetery until November 1883. All of Kent Ingall's classmates went to the grave that Memorial Day to place the annual flowers.
3. Ibid.
4. Henry Hurt, "Home of the Brave," *Reader's Digest*, May 1994. The author and Mr. Hurt exchanged several dozen e-mails and letters over several weeks starting in September 2015.
5. Henry Hurt, telephone interview by author on September 12, 2015. Mr. Hurt, was very helpful in filling in a number of details about Jerome Peirce's life based on the notes he still retained from his research for the *Reader's Digest* article. He also shared copies of the pictures of Peirce and his wife and daughter and made available copies of a few of the letters Peirce had written home.
6. Military Service Record for Jerome Peirce. Widow's Pension File for Albinia Peirce. Both sets of documents are maintained at the National Archives, Washington D.C. Both files were very complete. Sergeant Peirce's service record included 14 Company Muster Roles as well as his Enlistment/Discharge Certificate. The pension file Albinia's Claim for Widow's Pension, the Claim for Widow's Pension, several Widow's Claim for an Increase of Pension, and a certification of Albinia being dropped from the pension roles upon her death. Also included were documents such as proof of marriage and their daughter's birth certificate. Using the Ancesty.com databases, the author reviewed all of the U.S. Census enumeration forms from 1840 through 1940 that listed Jerome, Albinia, and Lucy Peirce. Several Commonwealth of Massachusetts census records were reviewed as well, as were a number of city directories for towns in Massachusetts, to determine where members of the Peirce and Jaquith families resided at various times.
7. Ibid. The dates of birth and dates of death in the documentation were found to be consistent with the inscriptions on the family gravestone in the Billerica cemetery.
8. History of the Thirty-Sixth Regiment Massachusetts Volunteers. 1862-

1865. (Boston: Rockwell and Churchill, 1884), pp. 368-373. The Roster of Enlisted Men for Company H notes such things as age at enlistment, hometown, and date mustered into U.S. service. If a soldier was killed, the roster includes the date and place of death.

9. The funeral service for Jerome Peirce, which included the sermon by Rev. Levi Ballou, was held on June 19, 1864, at the First Congregational Parish and Society Church in Orange, Massachusetts. The text of the service was located in the Rare Books and Special Collections Department of the Hesburgh Libraries of the University of Notre Dame, Notre Dame, Indiana.

10. *Thirty-Sixth Regiment,* pp. 1-36.

11. Ibid., pp. 37-134.

12. Jerome Peirce to Albinia Peirce, letter, April 26, 1864. This letter was written by Jerome Peirce while in camp in Alexandria, Virginia, approximately two weeks before he as killed. The original document is among the correspondence and photographs in the possession of Patricia Mason, great-grandniece of Albinia Peirce, in Dayton, Ohio.

13. *Thirty-Sixth Regiment,* p. 156.

14. Ibid. pp. 160-162.

15. Lt. Philip G. Woodward to Albinia Peirce, letter, July 4, 1864. The original is among the correspondence and photographs in the possession of Patricia Mason, in Dayton, Ohio.

16. Peirce Pension file.

17. The condition of the battlefield after the war and the removal of bodies to the National Cemetery are detailed in an unpublished book (written 2007) by National Park Service historian Donald C. Pfanz. It is called *Where Valor Proudly Sleeps: A History of Fredericksburg National Cemetery, 1866-1933* and a copy is available at the Fredericksburg and Spotsylvania National Military Park. Don Pfanz also wrote a related article for this journal called "'Skeleton Hunt:' The Burial of Union Dead in the Wilderness and at Spotsylvania Court House," *Fredericksburg History and Biography* (Fredericksburg, Virginia: Central Virginia Battlefields Trust, 2005).

18. Pfanz, *Where Valor Proudly Sleeps.* Some evidence about the location of Peirce's initial burial is found in Volume 25 of the *Roll of Honor,* which is a listing of soldiers interred in National Cemeteries and published in 1870. The entry for Sergeant Peirce reads: "McCool's Farm,

Spottsylvania County, Va." The McCoull house, built in 1846, was a prominent battlefield landmark and provides a good general location of where Peirce was killed and buried. Pfanz, "Skeleton Hunt," pp. 38-39.

19. Pfanz, "Skeleton Hunt," pp. 41-42.
20. Pfanz, *Where Valor Proudly Sleeps*.
21. Sergeant Jerome Peirce obituary, *The Bunker Hill Aurora and Boston Mirror* (Boston, MA), June 25, 1864.
22. Lucy Peirce's education and employment history are located at the Schlesinger Library at Radcliffe College, Harvard University.
23. An obituary ran for Andrew Birdsall in *The Free Lance* (Fredericksburg, Virginia) on February 23, 1897. The Birdsall obituary from a Massachusetts newspaper quoted here is an original newspaper clipping in the archives of the Fredericksburg and Spotsylvania National Military Park. The clipping, however, does not include the name of the newspaper, which was probably one from the Boston area.
24. Albinia Peirce obituary, *The Christian Register* (Boston, Massachusetts), March 18, 1920. Lucy Peirce obituary, *The Newton Graphic* (Newton, Massachusetts), August 15, 1946. U.S. Census, 1930, 1940.
25. *The Free Lance* (Fredericksburg, Virginia), July 26, 1892. U.S. Congress, *An Act to Establish and Protect National Cemeteries*, 39th Congress, February 22, 1867.
26. The Birdsall daughters all lived in Fredericksburg. They included Bessie Loreen (Birdsall) Moon, died before 1926; Augusta (Birdsall) Smith, died August 8, 1928; Florence (Birdsall) Heflin, died August 25, 1941; and Mabel Wicks (Birdsall) Gouldman, died December 26, 1964.
27. Superintendent Andrew Birdsall diary. The original is archived at the Fredericksburg and Spotsylvania National Military Park.
28. Bankbook for the Peirce Birdsall Memorial Fund, from The Farmers and Merchants State Bank of Fredericksburg, Virginia. Original is archived at the Fredericksburg and Spotsylvania National Military Park.
29. Ibid. No records have been found to indicate when or where the original $100 might have been deposited in a bank account. The bankbook entries begin October 8, 1919 and end on September 29, 1956. The disposition of this account after 1956 is also not clear. It may have been transferred into an interest-bearing bank account held by the National Park Service and designated for the perpetual care of local memorials. In August 2005, the great-granddaughters of Superintendent Birdsall

made a $500 contribution to the National Park Service to be used for decorating Sergeant Peirce's grave as well as the graves of Andrew and Julia Birdsall every Memorial Day. This donation was deposited into the "perpetual care account" by the National Park Service, with the consent of the Birdsall family descendants. In practice, the flowers in recent years have been procured and placed on Sergeant Peirce's grave by J. Gary Ingalls, Kent Ingalls' father, and his family without withdrawing funds from that account. According to Ingalls, who is a great-great-grandson of Andrew and Julia Birdsall, the graves of the Birdsalls have not been decorated for Memorial Day in recent years.

30. Any Satterthwaite, "Thanks for a promise kept: A Memorial Day tradition draws strangers' praise, *The Free Lance-Star* (Fredericksburg, Virginia), December 27, 1993.
31. Alice Heflin Abernathy obituary, *The Free Lance-Star* (Fredericksburg, Virginia), September 1, 1999.
32. Amy Satterthwaite, "Devotion to tradition touches family," *The Free Lance-Star* (Fredericksburg, Virginia), May 30, 1994.
33. Jennifer Strobel, "Lest we forget," *The Free Lance-Star* (Fredericksburg, Virginia), May 24, 2001.
34. J. Gary Ingalls, numerous telephone interviews with the author over the course of 2015.
35. Lucy Lawliss, Superintendent of the Fredericksburg and Spotsylvania National Military Park, to Michael P. Stevens, President of the Central Virginia Battlefields Trust, e-mail, August 5, 2015.

The Landram farm has become part of the Fredericksburg and Spotsylvania National Military Park. This view is from the ridge where the Landram farmhouse stood, looking toward the Bloody Angle.

THE FOLLOWING ARTICLE WAS PUBLISHED IN THE KNOXVILLE (TENNESSEE) *DAILY JOURNAL AND TRIBUNE*, ON JULY 21, 1895. ANNOTATIONS AND PHOTOS PROVIDED BY THE EDITORIAL STAFF OF *FREDERICKSBURG HISTORY AND BIOGRAPHY*.

AT SPOTTSYLVANIA
Mr. Beadle at the Scene of a Bloody Battle

Interviews With Local Residents—The Bloody Angle—General Grant's "Hammering" Process—A Few Comments on Grant and McClellan

(Special Correspondence)

SPOTTSYLVANIA COURT HOUSE, Va., July 15 – "You are now in the northeast corner of the bloody angle," said my host Mr. E. L. Landram, "though our fellows called it the bloody bend.—The McCool house just back there was the main center of the angle, and beginning at this pine tree, off that way for a hundred yards or so, the ditch was filled three deep with the dead.—You see, the Yankees broke over and were then driven back, and for awhile both sides fought over the same breastworks until some of our batteries got the range of the Yankees' side, and as the cannon shot swept along down it our fellows could hear the crash as they splintered the Yankees' bones.—I have often heard my uncle say it sounded just like it would if you had thrown a big rock into a pile of glass and china.—And every time the battery swept the ditch there was a scream, and the whole pile writhed and twisted like a pile of worms.—Our fellows say that men were just like devils that day—didn't care for life, their own or anybody else's.—They charged right up against the cannon and fought hand to hand and knocked each other down with their guns."[1]

Death and Destruction

"And where were you?"

"Oh, we had warning and ran down to the Court House.—I was only 12 years old then.—Our house was first taken for a Confederate hospital, and when the Confederates fell back and the Federals came on the whole place was swept clean.—All the horses were run off or killed, and a big herd of cattle were killed and everything else in the live stock line.—Our house was shot all to pieces, and the furniture destroyed and the fragments taken to build breastworks, but the strangest thing was about the feather beds.—When my sister and I came back, we walked along the breastworks, and she saw a piece of the ticking sticking out, so we went to work and dug and pulled and got every one of our seven feather beds out of the breastworks.—What the Yankees put them in for I can't imagine, but right along there, though it wasn't the hardest fighting, you could walk 100 yards or so on dead bodies.—This pine thicket was then an open field, but it has grown up thick enough since.—All this field was a graveyard.—The first years I

This ad is from the 1871 Richmond catalog of Southern Agricultural Works, printed by H.M. Smith and Company. As noted in this article, farmers needed to reclaim the scarred land to make a living and this post-war marketing tapped into that reality.

worked the farm I plowed up six skeletons.—Visitors from the north took them away as relics.—It is a little curious that where visitors used to come at the rate of 1,000 a year or more they stopped all at once a few years ago, and now there is hardly ever one.—I thought some of making a sort of tavern and trying to entertain visitors, but it won't do now.—The man who had the place the first year after father's death plowed down all the breastworks

The Landram homestead is marked by a reconstructed chimney base. Federal earthworks remain intact in the woods to the right.

in the fields, and some that was timber then has been cleared and the lines plowed down, and I am now very sorry that was done.—Now you can't follow the lines unless you have some one who knows them well."[2]

I found it true that I could trace no regular line.—In the woods the breastworks are still intact and trees have grown upon them a foot in thickness, with great masses of brush and tangled vines.—The interior breastwork, constructed by the Confederates after an entire division of them had been captured at the out angle, is now scarcely visible at all.—Striking westward from the McCool house on a sandy ridge where the land was so poor that it would make a western man sore eyed, I found a little the worst looking negro settlement I have yet seen in Virginia.—It was, in fact, the old plantation quarters, but the mansion of the master long ago disappeared, and the cabins look as if they were sinking into the earth.—I ventured to the door of one and found it dark inside as the den of a wild beast.[3]

Relics of the Conflict

The negroes were so stupid that I could understand them only with great difficult, but they had a curiosity to show me what they had recently plowed up—a human jaw and arm bone.—The jaw was one of enormous size, and nearly all the teeth were in tolerable preservation.—Not far beyond Mr. G.W. Perry showed me an army medal or bronze badge recently found near his house.—A little scouring brought out the original inscription and a rude scratching, perhaps made by the owner.—On one side were the words, "Against rebellion, 1862," inclosing a starred shield on which was the word, "Union!" on the other side, "W.H. Jackson, Co. D, 19th Regiment, Mich. Vols., Somerset Co."—A few rods north of Mr. Perry's and perhaps 2 ½ miles northwest of the courthouse is the Sedgwick monument and there was the northwest corner of the bloody field of May 12, 1864.—General Sedgwick was killed on the 9th, but the awful slaughter of the 12th completely overshadowed minor engagements in which from 2,000 to 6,000 men were killed, wounded and captured.[4]

I was considerably moved by the pathetic story of Mrs. Catherine Trigg, who still lives on the battlefield and whose son was killed a few days after the battle by the explosion of a shell.—All the boys who had ventured back to the neighborhood were busy gathering shells which they opened for the powder, and sometimes lead, which they contained.—Finding it difficult to open a very large one in the usual way, young Trigg tried it with a hammer and cold chisel.—It exploded, and he was torn to pieces.[5]

"He was only 16 years old," said Mrs. Trigg, "and intended to go in the army if the war continued, but was cut off.—He and Mr. Landram had opened many and thought they could do it safely.—We hurried back right after the battle.—In fact, we followed on the heels of the army, for we knew there would be no more fighting, but the awful stench drove us away again.—There come on heavy rains, and after that nearly everybody was sick.—In fact, all the rest of that year was the sickliest ever known, for this is a very healthy country."[6]

A Lucky Individual

At one point was a Confederate regiment mostly from West Virginia, and of the company on the extreme left all were killed or wounded but one, as there was a sudden enfilading fire from the Federals.—Monroe Hansford, the lucky man, has had an extraordinary career and is still living.—I did not see him, but his brother gave me this account: "Well, I reckon if this world was to break in pieces Monroe Hansford would manage to get on the biggest and come out alive.—He has been mighty near death in every sort of way, by boats sinking or exploding and in shooting and cutting scrapes, and in the Wilderness he put up his own headstone and lived to tell it.— They were ordered to lie down till the Yankees came close up, and the lower half of his body was in a little gully.—Seeing a big flat stone near him, he picked it up and held it edgeways just in front of his head.—It was struck by six or seven rifle bullets, and the men to the right and left of him, three or four each way, were killed and all the rest wounded, but he escaped."[7]

The Sedgwick monument was put up on the 12th of May, 1887, and for three days a large concourse of survivors of the old Sixth corps rambled over the various battlefields in the vicinity.—All the neighbors with whom I talked did not fail to inform me that the Battlefield association paid Mrs. Owens $50 for the acre on which the monument stands, which is from 5 to 50 times as much as the current price of land anywhere in the region.—All the historians say that no one can understand these Wilderness battles or comprehend the reasons for Grant's attack on May 12 unless he comes here and studies the ground.—Well, for myself only I must say that after walking all over the field I can see how they fought, but as to reasons for this battle I know what I did before—just nothing at all.—I do not wonder that popular opinion through all this section of Virginia in unanimous in regard to the Federal commander.—This was the last battle save one in which he hurled his veterans headlong on strong breastworks manned by expert riflemen.[8]

A Remarkable Fact.
The "hammering' process, of which some writers still speak approvingly, was begun May 4 by order of General Grant and terminated June 3 by order of his soldiers.—It last just 30 days, and the Federal losses averaged 2,000 per day.—The Virginia estimate, therefore, is that had the policy been continued it would have cost 300,000 men to take Richmond.—Measured, however, by the time in action the loss per hour increased at an almost geometrical ratio.—Thus at the last desperate charge of the so called Wilderness series twice as many men were lost as in the first; at Laurel Hill the loss was doubled again, at the bloody angle doubled again and at Cold Harbor the loss was between 8,000 and 9,000 in half an hour, or at the rate of 17,000 per hour.—Then, the only case recorded in history so far as I know, a whole

The Sedgwick monument was put up on the 12th of May, 1887, and for three days a large concourse of survivors of the old Sixth corps rambled over the various battlefields in the vicinity.

Fredericksburg Mayor Joseph Hazard greeted the Union veterans who arrived by train to dedicate the Sedgwick monument.

army without previous understanding unanimously refused obedience.—The order for another charge was given, repeated by corps and division commanders and so on down the line of officers.—The trumpets sounded the charge.—The whole army stood still.—It should not be forgotten that it was not the general who stopped the "hammering" process by his own will.—It was the private soldiers who did it, and a most remarkable and dramatic circumstance it was.

McClellan reached the James river with a loss of 19,000 and inflicted a lost of 21,000 on Lee.—Grant reached the same place with a loss of 60,000 men, inflicting a loss of 23,000 on Lee.—At that point both proposed the same plan.—In 1862 is was rejected and in 1864 is was accepted.—McClellan did not venture to promise that Richmond could be taken by his plan in less than six months, and his proposition was ridiculed accordingly.—Grant did it in nine months.—If this were all, we could quickly decide the old contention as to relative rank of the commanders of the Army of the Potomac, but there is a deal more.—Grant was always respectful to his superiors, McClellan often grossly insulting and generally contemptuous.—Our civil war cannot be judged by old world standards, for the political fights were, if possible, even more important than the military.—The administration could drive on the soldiers or trust bulldog general to do so, but it had to satisfy men who supported the war.—In 1861 and 1862 these men were fiercely impatient of delay and timid as to loss of life, taxation and expenditures.—In 1864 they were in the humor to spend every dollar, sacrifice every man and to go to any length necessary in winding up the job.   —J.H. BEADLE

NOTES

1. E.L. Landram refers to Edward L. Landram. The Landram homestead stood within the Federal lines, northeast of what would be called the Bloody Angle. Major General Winfield Scott Hancock occupied it as his Second Corps headquarters during the fighting on May 12, 1864. The McCoull house stood within the Confederate salient.
2. Civil War battlefields went through various stages. The armies dug trenches and earthworks and sometimes buried at least a portion of the dead. Post-war, property owners reclaimed their fields by filling in earthworks and removing bodies. In time, some places were acquired and preserved as historic sites, while many others were developed. When this article was written, the numbers of visitors to the battlefield had likely dropped off due to an economic recession. In addition, a National Battlefield Park was being established at Gettysburg in 1895, which drew visitors away from other sites they may have otherwise travelled to see.
3. This area could be the Harrison farm, which stood on a ridge at the base of the Confederate salient.
4. G.W. Perry was George Washington Perry, a local Spotsylvania County resident. The information scratched into the army medal found by the African American farmer may have been difficult to read. The roster for the 19th Michigan Infantry does not show a W.H. Jackson for Company D. There was, however, a G.W. Jackson in Company C. The state may also have been difficult to read and the unit may well have been from a state other than Michigan. The casual racism expressed by the writer is disturbing and ugly. In 1895, African Americans were being denied basic rights, including education, and lived a difficult existence.
5. A certain percentage of artillery rounds fired in wartime do not explode, typically due to a fuze malfunction. The main charge within the shell, however, remains an explosive hazard, even years after the fact. Casualties of any past war can still result from mishandling still-live artifacts.
6. Further details of the conditions found on the battlefield immediately after the war can be found in an article by Donald C. Pfanz called "'Skeleton Hunt:' The Burial of Union Dead in the Wilderness and at Spotsylvania Court House," *Fredericksburg History and Biography* (Fredericksburg, Virginia: Central Virginia Battlefields Trust, 2005).

7. There was a Private Monroe Hansford in the 8th Virginia Cavalry and some of that unit's companies included soldiers from West Virginia. There are no further details, however, to confirm whether that person and the person referred to in this article are, in fact, the same person.
8. The Sedgwick monument is an impressive granite edifice that stands nine feet tall. It was commissioned and funded by veterans of the Sixth Corps, who formed the Sedgwick Memorial Association in 1887. The Battlefield Association mistakenly called out in the article is the Chancellorsville Battlefield Association, which had formed in 1891 and had begun to acquire land at Chancellorsville as well as at Spotsylvania Court House. This latter enterprise eventually dissolved and all of the battlefield land it had acquired had to be relinquished. The dedication ceremony for the Sedgwick memorial was attended by 300 veterans who had arrived in Fredericksburg by rail the day before and been welcomed by Mayor Josiah Hazard. Hundreds more local citizens attended the dedication as well.

Major General John M. Schofield, Military Governor of the First Military District, which was set up to supervise Virginia under the Reconstruction Act of 1867. In 1868, he appointed Charles E. Mallam, a former Union officer, to be Fredericksburg's mayor, replacing the long-serving wartime mayor and local resident Montgomery Slaughter.

Minutes of the Common Council of the Town of Fredericksburg, 1868-1869

TYPESCRIPT CORRECTED AND ANNOTATED BY ERIK F. NELSON

Although the Civil War ended in 1865, an intensely rancorous political struggle continued into the post-war period. The former Confederate states, which had dominated the U.S. Congress in the decades prior to the war, sought to regain as much of their former political hegemony as possible. The U.S. government, on the other hand, wanted to be sure that the goals achieved in war would not be lost in peace. The tense period of Reconstruction played out in a nation already irrevocably changed, even as the South tried to cling to its old social order as much as possible.

The abolition of slavery was the most significant outcome of the war and the political impact of several million newly-freed African Americans bubbled up as the most immediate factor in how the two warring sections of the nation would interact. The pre-war tensions were not ended at Appomattox. The U.S. Constitution had counted slaves as three-fifths of a person, a necessary compromise to establish a new nation following the American Revolution. The Southern states had thus gained a level of representation in Congress that allowed it to dominate that legislative body, while keeping a significant part of the population they seemingly represented in bondage. With former slaves now become full persons, the South's Congressional representation would increase, potentially reestablishing the conditions that had led to war.

At issue was whether African Americans would be able to vote. The Republican Party had a strong interest in that large segment of the population that would most likely vote Republican. The South's white population was strongly Democrat and wanted the advantages of the increased representation, without having to allow the former slaves to affect the election results. The emerging power in this post-war struggle was a faction of Republicans described as Radical.

When the war began, the U.S. government had been limited in its ability to handle the crisis. To successfully prosecute the war, the central government established as a coalition of states grew in scope to become a truly national government. A military force of previously unimaginable size and power had been raised and supported through a vastly enhanced financial system and an industrialized economy that included hundreds of new factories, integrated railroads, and a telegraph network. The federal bureaucracy had also grown substantially to handle the many new responsibilities

The seceding Southern states had left a Republican Congress able to enact a great many new things as well as legislation that had previously been blocked. Without Southern representatives to vote against them, the wartime Republicans established a strong industrial economy through a proper financial system, paper money, and a new system of taxation. They passed the Land Grant College Act, to assist states to set up institutions that would train emerging generations to be successful in agricultural and mechanical pursuits. They enacted the Homestead Act to help settle western lands. They facilitated railroad development, including a transcontinental link. This strong federal activity had also been mobilized against slavery and would continue to be used in its aftermath.

The Republican Congress had also ensured passage of two amendments to the Constitution. The Thirteenth Amendment abolished slavery in the United States. The Fourteenth Amendment established a national citizenship, whose rights could not be deprived by any state. Former Confederate states would be required to ratify these amendments as a condition for readmission to the Union and many states balked. In January 1867, for instance, the General Assembly of the Commonwealth of Virginia rejected rather that ratified the Fourteenth Amendment.

Southern factions were too often unwilling to concede that their world had changed. They engaged in a concerted violence to keep former slaves from thinking they had rights, which caused a growing concern in the North that translated into votes. As a consequence, the 1866 elections gave the Republicans a strong majority in Congress. In July 1867, the new Congress responded to Southern intransigence and increasing racial violence by passing the Reconstruction Act. President Andrew Johnson, who wanted to declare the Civil War goals achieved, vetoed the bill, but an angry Republican Congress overrode the President's opposition. They began their version of Reconstruction by establishing martial law over the defeated South. Under Congressional Reconstruction, the South was divided into five military districts, under which state governments would be reconstituted. The U.S. Army would also supervise local governments while protecting the African American population.

In the pages that follow, we see Fredericksburg's elected representatives engaged in the usual local issues such as considering gas street lights, dealing with a residual lawlessness, and seeking to generate needed revenues. In the spring of 1868, however, we see the beginning of martial law. So far, the Southern political landscape had not changed much and post-war Southern legislatures looked very much like the pre-war legislatures. In Fredericksburg, the local populace was not pleased that newly free African Americans thought they would be able to participate in the electoral process as equals. Local papers reflect a strong paternalism and expectation that the better educated and more experienced white men were best able to represent the interests of the black population (eg. Virginia Herald, 18 March 1867).

The Radical Republicans were not about to let the old guard remain in place. The very active Civil War Congress had passed a law in the summer of 1862 over the objection of President Abraham Lincoln that required federal bureaucrats to take an oath that they had not taken up arms against their government and also had not supported those who did. This rule is referred to in the Fredericksburg Common Council minutes as the Act of Congress passed July 2, 1862 and it comes up frequently. The required oath was also known as the iron-clad oath and the Republicans in Congress used it to remove former Confederates and Confederate sympathizers from the political process. The impact of this active Reconstruction had come to Fredericksburg in March 1867, when local elections were suspended, and in early 1868 the Federals imposed martial law before allowing elections to proceed. The two years featured in this year's Journal show the local government coping with this continuation of the Civil War into peacetime.

The Council minutes are handwritten documents in handsomely bound volumes. In addition to this record copy, there are also rough drafts, written as the Council was in session. During the Great Depression, the Works Progress Administration hired people to type out the handwritten minutes, which are available in several locations for research. The WPA workers, however, did not get into the first drafts and thus did not find where words and sometimes entire paragraphs had been missed by whoever had copied out the minutes smooth. The transcribed minutes published by the CVBT include these missing sections, which are identified by brackets. This additional information includes missing data, but sometimes just reflects minor differences in wording. Either way, this published document is as complete as it is possible to be.

1868

At a regular meeting of the Common Council of the Town of Fred[ericks]b[ur]g held at the Council Chamber, on Tuesday [the] 28th Jany. 1868. at 7 P.M.

Present– M. Slaughter, Mayor
J.G. Hurkamp, Jas. W. Sener, W.A. Little, E.M. Braxton, Geo. W. Wroten, Jas. H. Bradley, A.P. Rowe, Wm. H. Cunningham, Jas. McGuire, Jno. J. Young.

On motion made & seconded, St. Geo. R. Fitzhugh, Esq. presented to the Council a proposition from Mr. J.B. Ficklen offering the sum of five thousand dollars in the bonds of the Corporation for the fee simple title to the house & lot on Main Street now held by him on a lease for lives.

On motion of Mr. E.M. Braxton, as Attorney for the parties, ordered that the Collector of taxes be instructed to settle their ground rents now due and to become due by D. Green's Estate, by receiving the past due coupons of the Corporation in payment thereof.

Mr. Wm. A. Little moved the following resolution–

Resolved that the Pub[lic] Prop[erty] Committee be instructed to advertise for 20 days for proposals to purchase in the Corporation Bonds, the lots on Market Square in which the Corporation now holds the reversion & the 10 acres known as the Mercer Square & failing to make said sale privately, they be, and they are hereby instructed at the expiration of said time to sell the same at Public auction–Subject to the confirmation of the Council - Which Mr. Bradley moved to amend by inserting the words "for Cash or" after the word purchase–and the amendment being seconded the question was taken & the amendment was lost. The question then recurred on the original resolution of Mr. Little and it was adopted.[1]

The Mayor then presented a communication from Robt. Walker and J.F. Smith preferring a complaint against Martin Cahill & Chas W. Edrington, two of the night police, and on motion Mr. Walker & Mr. Smith were heard by the Council, Mr. Mazeen was also heard & likewise Mr. Cahill & Mr. Edrington. Mr. J.B. Sener appeared as Counsel for Messrs. Walker & Smith & was heard by the Council.

Mr. J.H. Bradley moved that the action of the Night policemen, Cahill & Edrington, in the matter complained of by Messrs. Walker & Smith, be sustained by the Council, which being seconded, the motion was adopted.

A bill of Johnston & Co. against the Corporation amounting to $2.43 was passed and order'd to be paid.

Mr. J.W. Sener called up the report submitted to the Council in Jany. 1867 by a committee appointed to ascertain the cost of lighting the Streets of the town with gas, & asked that the report might be read again, which was accordingly done.[2]

A bill of the Fredericksburg Ledger, for printing the delinquent list amounting to $72.00 was read and Mr. Braxton moved that it be paid. Mr. Huffman, Mr. Little & Mr. Sener were heard on the matter, when the Council, after a division, the Mayor giving the casting vote, refused [to pay] the bill.

Mr. McGuire moved that the bill be referred to the Finance Committee for report, which motion was lost.

On motion of Mr. A.P. Rowe, Ordered that the sum of $64.80 be paid the Editor of the Fredericksburg Ledger in full for printing the delinquent list.

On motion of Mr. E.M. Braxton, ordered that the Street Commission be directed to fill up the well at the corner of A.K. Phillips' lot on Main Street.

On motion of Mr. Wm. H. Cunningham–

Resolved that a Committee of three be appointed to confer with the Gas Company & with the Citizens of the Town & ascertain if an arrangement can be made by which the Town can be properly lighted & the Corporation relieved of the expense of lamp posts & other fixtures & report to a meeting of the Council to be held by next Tuesday evening. Committee, Wm. H. Cunningham, Jas. H. Bradley & Jas W. Sener.

And [then] the Council adjourned till Tuesday next, the 4th day of Feby. at 7 P.M.

[M. Slaughter, Mayor]

At an adjourned meeting of the Common Council of the town of Fredericksburg held at the Council Chamber on Tuesday evening the 4th day of February 1868.

Present– M. Slaughter, Mayor

T.F. Knox, Recorder

J.G. Hurkamp, Wm. A. Little, Jas. H. Bradley, Geo. W. Wroten, E.M. Braxton, Wm. H. Cunningham, Jno. J. Young, Ab. P. Rowe, Jas. McGuire, J.W. Sener.

The Mayor stated that this was an adjourned meeting of the Council to receive the report of the Committee, appointed to confer with the citizens & with the Gas Company as to lighting the streets of the Town.

Mr. Wm. H. Cunningham, (Chairman of the Gas Co.), presented a report in writing, accompanied by a plan for the position of the lamps, in words and figures following, to wit, viz:

The Committee appointed to confer with the Gas Company, and with the Citizens of the Town, upon the subject of lighting the streets with Gas, beg leave to report, that having conferred with the President of the Gas Co., they were led to believe, that immediately on the use of the gas by the Corporation to the extent of the Consumption twenty five or more lamps, the price of Gas would be reduced to all consumers from its present price of six to four dollars p[e]r thousand feet, and the President stated that he would immediately call a meeting of the Gas Co[mpany] to authorize this arrangement, which has been accomplished, as will appear by reference to accompanying report of [the] proceedings of the Gas Company at their meeting on the 30th ultimo. This arrangement having been stated to the Citizens, generally property holders & business men of the Town, we found them [almost] universally disposed to contribute to the purchase of lamps & other fixtures necessary to the town being properly lighted, and in some cases it was stated that if the amount contributed was not sufficient, an additional amount would be given, it being considered that the success of the movement was highly important to the interests of the Town, having entirely out of view personal Comfort and Convenience. The amount already subscribed is Eleven Hundred & fifteen dollars ($1115) & subscriptions from the Steamboat Company [Companies] & other parties are confidently expected, Accompanying is a plan proposed [prepared] by the Committee for the arranging the lamp posts proposed to be used, which have been prepared with care & which they recommend for your adoption. This plan involves the use of 32 lamps and posts, three of which are already furnished, One by the Episcopal, One by the Methodist Church & One by the Exchange Hotel. The cost of the necessary fixtures is estimated as follows:

1075 feet of surface pipe ¾ inch @	.25	268.75
29 Lamp posts	11.	319.00
29 Lamps	6.	174.00
29 Burners	1.00	29.00
29 Fittings	about	8.00
Digging, setting & paving for posts		60.00
		858.75

The Committee would state that the arrangements made with the Gas Co[mpany] by which a large reduction in the price of Gas is made to all Consumers, was urged not only on the ground of a large consumption by the Corporation which will scarcely equal the amount of reduction, but also on the ground of a large increase of Consumption at the reduced price on the part of the Citizens of the Town, & it is hoped by your Committee, who are not in any manner identified with the Gas Co[mpany] that the Citizens generally will now use the gas, and thus ensure the continuance of an arrangement which we think will prove beneficial to all parties.

    Respectfully Submitted,
    Wm. H. Cunningham
    Jas. H. Bradley
    J.W. Sener

Which on motion of Mr. Jno. J. Young were adopted.

Mr. Wm. H. Cunningham moved that the vote adopting the report of the Gas Committee be reconsidered which being seconded, the vote was taken & resulted in the affirmative, so the vote was reconsidered.

On motion, Mr. Wm. H. Cunningham again read the report of the Gas Committee, when Mr. A.P. Rowe offered the following as a substitute therefor, Viz:

Whereas it appears to the Common Council of the Town of Fred[ericks]burg that a portion of the Citizens are very desirous that the streets of said town shall be lighted with gas, And whereas in the present condition of the Corporation Treasury, the inability of the said Corporation to meet its interest obligations, and the poverty of a portion of the people (being such as to require a large portion of real estate to be offered for sale for the taxes due thereon) entirely preclude the Council from inflicting any further tax on the people at this time for lighting said Streets with gas, – Therefore, be it ordained by the Mayor & Common Council, that it shall be lawful for any person or persons to erect lamp posts, for either gas or oil, on the streets of this Corporation, under the supervision of the Street Committee, providing [that] said posts shall not obstruct the streets & footways, & provided also that the parties erecting the said posts, shall pay all the expense of said posts and for all gas or oil consumed by said lamps, Which being seconded, before the vote was taken, Mr. Sener presented a report showing the expense of lighting the streets with Gas per lamp, when the question being taken on the substitute offered by Mr. Rowe, the Ayes & Noes were called for and resulted as follows:

Noes–Messrs. Knox, Hurkamp, Little, Bradley, Wroten, Braxton, Cunningham, Young & Sener   9

Ayes–Messrs. Rowe & McGuire   2

So the substitute was lost.

Mr. McGuire then moved [that] the matter of lighting the streets with gas be referred to the people for a vote to be taken thereon, Which being seconded, the Ayes & Noes were called for and resulted as follows:

Noes–Messrs. Knox, Hurkamp, Little, Bradley, Wroten, Braxton, Cunningham, Young & Sener   9

Ayes–Messrs. Rowe & McGuire   2

So the motion was lost.

On motion of Mr. Wm. A. Little, the report of the Committee on Gas, with the plan accompanying, was received and adopted.

The following resolutions offered by Mr. Wm. A. Little were adopted:

1st Resolved that Wm. H. Cunningham, Jas. H. Bradley & Jas. W. Sener, be and they are hereby appointed a permanent Committee upon Gas and that they be & they are hereby instructed to collect the subscriptions & contract for the work of purchasing and putting up the lamp posts and other fixtures and carrying out the plan submitted in this report.

2nd Resolved, that said Committee be instructed to have said work done as far as possible by our own mechanics in Fredericksburg.

And [then] the Council adjourned.

[M. Slaughter, Mayor]

At a Regular Meeting of the Common Council of the Town of Fred[ericks]burg. held at the Council Chamber on Tuesday the 25th day of Feb[ruar]y 1868.

Present– M. Slaughter, Mayor
        Thos. F. Knox, Recorder
Wm. A. Little, Ab. P. Rowe, Geo. W. Wroten, Jas. H. Bradley, Jno. G. Hurkamp & Jas W. Sener.

The Mayor presented a communication from Mr. W.J. Jefferies in regard to the booth at the Corner of Commerce & Main Streets, when Mr. Bradley moved that Mr. Jefferies be allowed to occupy the said booth at the pleasure of the Council, which motion was lost.[3]

Mr. A.P. Rowe moved to reconsider the vote by which the application of Mr. Jefferies was rejected, which was carried.

On motion of Mr. J.G. Hurkamp, Ordered that Mr. Jefferies be allowed to occupy the booth at the Corner of Commerce & Main Streets, during the pleasure of the Council, provided that he obtain the consent in writing of a majority of the property holders and tenants in that square and files the same with the Clerk of the Council.

And then the Council adjourned.
        [M. Slaughter, Mayor]

At a called meeting of the Common Council of the Town of Fred[erick]sburg, held at the Council Chamber on Friday evening March 6th, 1868.

Present– M. Slaughter, Mayor
        Thos. F. Knox, Recorder
Wm. A. Little, Jas. W. Sener, Jas. H. Bradley, Geo. W. Wroten, E.M. Braxton and Wm. H. Cunningham.

The Mayor stated that this was a called meeting of the Council to receive a report from the Public Property Committee, but as the Chairman of that Committee was not present, the Council proceeded to other business.

Mr. J.B. Sener, by consent of the Council, called the attention of the Council to the fact that Dr. Sears, the Chairman of the Peabody Educational Committee, was now distributing the funds appropriated by Mr. Peabody for the cause of Education in the South, Whereupon on motion of Mr. Bradley -

Resolved that the Mayor & Chamberlain be appointed a Committee on the part of the Council to correspond with Dr. Sears and obtain from him the facts in regard to the distribution of the Peabody fund.[4]

Present– Jas. McGuire & Ab. P. Rowe

Mr. Jas. W. Sener, by note in writing, tendered his resignation as a member of the Gas Committee, which on motion was laid on the table.

Mr. Jas. W. Sener, was excused from further attendance at this Council.

Absent– J.W. Sener

Mr. McGuire, Chairman Pub. Prop. Comtee, submitted a report in writing, in the words and figures following, to wit

The P.P. Committee, who were charged by resolution of your Honorable body of the [blank] day of January, with the sale of certain property therein mentioned, beg leave respectfully to report, that as the sale was to be made, subject to the confirmation of the Council, they determined to let it go to the highest bidder, without any [other] reservation & the following is the result, Viz:

The house occupied by Jas. L. Green was knocked down to Ab. P. Rowe payable in Corporation Bonds at

$4,000.00

That occupied by S. Hirsh to J.B. Ficklen	7,000.00
Mercer Square to Dr. Wm. S. Scott	6,100.00

The latter property had been divided into ¼ acre lots (see accompanying map) and was put up as an entity, reserving the right to annul, and sell in lots, but the limited number of bidders present, determined your Committee to report as above.[5]

   Respectfully submitted
   Jas. McGuire
   E.M. Braxton
   Geo. W. Wroten

which report was on motion received.

On motion of Mr. Bradley, resolved that the sales reported by the Pub. Prop. Committee be not confirmed.

Mr. Bradley moved that the Pub. Prop. Committee be authorized to sell the house on Main Street occupied by J. Hirsh for $8,500, the house occupied by J.L. Green for $6,500, and the Mercer Square for $9,000, payable in Corporation bonds, the refusal to be given to the highest bidder, at the sale reported today, the said Committee to report to the next meeting of the Council, which motion was adopted.

And then the Council adjourned.

[M. Slaughter, Mayor]

At a meeting of the Common Council of the Town of Fredericksburg held at the Council Chamber on Tuesday the 24th day of March 1868.

Present– M. Slaughter, Mayor
Wm. H. Cunningham, Jas. H. Bradley, Geo. W. Wroten, E.M. Braxton, Jas. W. Sener, Jas. McGuire, Jno. G. Hurkamp, Thos. F. Knox, Recorder, Jno. J. Young.

The Mayor stated that this was a regular meeting of the Council & there being no reports from Committees, the Council proceeded to other business.

The Mayor presented a communication from Mr. Jas. Mazeen asking permission to erect a privy in the Market House Yard, which on motion was laid on the table.

The Mayor presented an application from Messrs, Waite & Sener asking the privilege of digging a well in rear of their store on Commerce Street for the purpose of making a sink, which on motion of Mr. Cunningham was referred to the Pub. Pro. Committee.[6]

The Mayor presented [an application] from G.A. Rawlett asking the Council to refund to him the amount paid by him for redemption for a hog caught running at large and sold under the ordinance of the Corporation, amounting to Six 50/100 dollars, which on motion of Mr. Braxton was granted and the Chamberlain was ordered to pay the said amount ($6.50) to Mr. Rawlett.

On motion of Mr. Wroten, Ordered that the Chamberlain refund to Mr. P.B. Dunn One 75/100 Doll[ar]s the amt. for which a Hog belonging to him & caught running at large, was sold under an ordinance of the Corporation.

Mr. E.M. Braxton presented a communication from Duff Green, Admnr. of D. Green Decd., in regard to the ground rent paid by him since the war in greenbacks amounting to $135.00, & on motion Mr. L.J. Huffman was heard, when on motion of Mr. J.W. Sener the communication was referred to the Finance Committee.[7]

A bill of Geo. Aler's for defending a suit against Wallace amtg. to

$25.00 & also certain fee bills of the Clerk amtg. to $6.49 were referred to Finance Committee.

Mr. Geo. W. Wroten presented a communication from Mr. Jas. L. Green asking to be relieved from a fine imposed upon him this day amounting to twenty dollars for hauling lumber in the Town of Fredericksburg without a license, & on motion Mr. L.J. Huffman was permitted to make a statement, which on motion of Mr. McGuire the communication was laid on the table.

On motion of Mr. Bradley the tax on Drays, Carts & Wagons from the 1st Ap[ri]l 1868 to 1st Ap[ri]l 1869 was fixed as follows, Viz: on Drays & Carts five Dollars, and on Wagons ten Dollars.

On motion of Mr. Jas. W. Sener, Ordered that the Police Officers notify all owners of property in the Corporation where pavements are out or order to repair the same within ten days from date of notice, & in the event that they fail to repair the same, that the Corporation will have it done, & the expense to be recovered by warrant.

On motion of Mr. McGuire, Ordered that the Claim of the Corporation against Dr. B.R. Wellford for repairs to the pavement in front of his house on Princess Anne Street, and all similar claims against other persons, be referred to the Finance Committee, with instructions to make the same.[8]

And then the Council adjourned.

[M. Slaughter, Mayor]

At a called meeting of the Common Council of the Town of Fred[erick]sburg, held at the Council Chamber on Saturday evening March 28th, 1868.

Present– M. Slaughter, Mayor
        Thos. F. Knox, Recorder
Wm. A. Little, Jas. McGuire, Jas. H. Bradley, Jas. W. Ford, George W. Wroten & Wm. H. Cunningham.

The Mayor stated the Council had been convened at the instance of several members to take into consideration the finances of the Corporation incidentally and more directly the questions of retaining the Night Watch in office.

On motion of Mr. Little, Ordered that on and after the 1st day of April next the number of Night Watch shall be reduced to two.

Present– J.G. Hurkamp.

The Council then proceeded to ballot for the two Night Watchmen to be retained and resulted as follows, Viz:

Chas. W. Edrington	6
M. Cahill	5
Geo. H. Timberlake	3
Jno. B. Larkin	1
F. W. Roberts	1

So Chas. W. Edrington & Martin Cahill were declared to be elected as Night Watch after the 1st day of April 1868, to serve during the pleasure of the Council.

Mr. Little presented and read to the Council a statement in regard to the action of the Council in appointing the Night Watch, which was adopted by the Council and ordered to be spread on the minutes, And the Clerk of the Council is ordered to prepare a copy of the said statement and enclose the same to Mr. Jno. L. Marye, Jr., at Richmond, with the request that he present the same to Genl. Schofield.[9]

The statement is as follows-
To Genl. Schofield
   Commanding Military District No. 1

The Common Council of Fredericksburg, Va., being informed that Lieut. H. Sears, who is an agent of the Freedman's Bureau in this place, has reported or is about to report to your Head Quarters the action of this body in appointing a Night Watch as a violation of your Genl. Order No. [blank] which requires all Officers hereafter qualifying to take the oath required by the Act of 1862, before entering on the duties of their offices, respectfully state that they have in no way violated said [Genl] Order as alleged. The robberies at night having increased to an alarming extent in the Town, the Council appointed five Citizens to act as a Night Watch, to patrol the Town at night and guard the property of the Citizens from these depredations. The Night Watch is paid per night and is removable at pleasure, they are in no sense Police Officers, give no bond & security & have no right to arrest, except the right which any other Citizen has to arrest a party engaged in violating the law & carry him before some Magistrate for examination & committal or discharge. Not regarding said Night Watch as Officers required by said Genl. Order to take the Oath referred to, they were not required to do so, & this action was understood to have been approved by Col. Johnson who was then in charge of the Freedmans Bureau's Offices here.[10]

Recently and on the night of the 24th inst. one of the Night Watch being present on the occasion, was directed by the Mayor to arrest a Negro, who was then very drunk & engaged in the actual violation of the laws in the presence of the Mayor. This order could as well and as lawfully been given to any private Citizen who happened to be present, as to a member of the Night Watch. And as it can hardly be maintained that the two constructions of said Genl. Order would require a Magistrate, before directing a citizen to aid in the arrest of a flagrant violation [violator] of the law in his very presence, to stop and wait until he administered the said oath to him, in order to qualify him to perform said duty, that [the] action of the Mayor in ordering said arrest by a member of the Night Watch, cannot be considered as making the said Night Watch a Police Officer, nor as violating said Genl. Order.

The Mayor and Council of Fredericksburg have endeavoured (sic) to the best of their ability to comply strictly with the laws of the land, and with all orders from those in authority, which in the present state of the Country, it was manifestly their duty to obey, and they respectfully challenge any investigation into their conduct in the past, which may be desired by any having Authority over such matters.

Ordered that the tax on Vehicles, other than drays, carts, & wagons, be fixed at the same rate as last year.

The use of the picks, shovels &c, belonging to the Corporation in the hands of the Superintendent of the Streets, was on motion given to the Committee on Gas to assist in putting up the lamp posts.

And then the Council adjourned.

[M. Slaughter, Mayor]

At a called meeting of the Common Council of the Town of Fredericksburg, held at the Council Chamber, on Friday evening, the 10th day of Ap[ri]l. 1868.

Present– M. Slaughter, Mayor
Wm. A. Little, Wm. H. Cunningham, Jas. [Joseph (sic)]W. Sener, Jno. G. Hurkamp, Jas. M. McGuire, E.M. Braxton, J.H. Bradley, Ab. P. Rowe.

The Mayor stated that the meeting had been called at the instance of two [or] three members to complete some unfinished business.

The following resolution offered by Mr. Jas. W. Sener was unanimously adopted, viz:

Resolved, that the Council hereby conveys all its rights & title to the Schooner now sunk in the harbor to Capt. John Williams, who is raising the Steam Boat wrecks, on condition that the said Schooner be removed so as not to obstruct or impair navigation.

The following resolution offered by Mr. J.H. Bradley was adopted.

Resolved, that the lamp posts, the lamps & fixtures purchased by private prescriptions and put up in the Streets of the Town, by permission of the Council, for the use of the Corporation in lighting the Streets, are now and shall remain the private property of the said private Contributors– Subject to the said use only of lighting said Streets, And that the Chairman of the Gas Committee is requested to deposit with the Clerk of the Council a list of all the said private contributors.

The [Chairman of the] Finance Committee reported adversely to the application of Duff Green, Execr. of Duff Green, Decd., which was referred to the Finance Comttee at the last meeting of the Council.

The Finance Committee having also reported adversely to the payment of a bill of Geo. Aler, referred to the Committee at the last meeting of the Council.

The Finance Committee having reported favorably, Ordered that the fee bills of J.J. Chew, Clerk, amounting to $6.47, be paid by the Chamberlain.

A bill of Jas. McGuire amounting to $5.25, was ordered to be paid.

On motion of Mr. Jas. McGuire, Resolved that Mr. Jas. L. Green be allowed to pay a fine adjudged against him of twenty dollars for hauling in the Corporation without a license, in the past due coupons of the Corporation, in consideration of the circumstances of the case.

A bill of A.P. Rowe against the Corporation amounting to twenty dollars was allowed by the Council and ordered to be paid.

And then the Council adjourned.

[M. Slaughter, Mayor]

Fredericksburg, Va., Ap[ri]l. 17th, 1868.

At a Meeting of the Common Council of the Town of Fredericksburg convened in obedience to instructions from Maj. Genl. Schofield, commanding this District, communicated through Lieut. G.G. Greenough, Military Commissioner, there were present the following old members of the Council, who held over under orders from Genl. Schofield, Viz:

Messrs. M. Slaughter, Mayor, Wm. A. Little, Wm. H. Cunningham, J.G. Hurkamp & Ab. P. Rowe.

And the following new members appointed by Genl. Schofield, Viz:

Chas. E. Hunter   Peter Couse[11]
Wm. C. Morrison   D.C. Ellis
L.C. Frost   Geo. W. Eve
W.J. Jefferies

appeared, were qualified by [before] the Mayor, by taking the oath required by the Act of Congress passed July 2nd 1862 & took their seats at the Board.

On motion of Mr. J.G. Hurkamp, Ordered that the salaries of all the Officers of the Corporation, who are appointed by the Council, be fixed at the same rates as at present.

The Council then proceeded to recommend to Genl. Schofield, a suitable person to be appointed Mayor of this Corporation to serve until his successor shall be duly elected and qualified, when Chas. E. Mallam & Geo. W. Eve being put in nomination, the vote was taken by ballot and resulted as follows, Viz:

For Chas. E. Mallam --------- Seven

An 1862 sketch by Edwin Forbes. The note reads: "Remains of burnt steamers & sailing vessels on the Rappahanock (sic)." The Fredericksburg town council needed to address these obstacles to renew their river trade, but had limited means to do so.

" Geo. W. Eve ---------------   Three

So Chas. E. Mallam was declared duly recommended.[12]

Not voting – Geo. W. Eve.

The Council then proceeded to recommend a suitable person for Recorder of this Corporation, when L.C. Frost, Esqr. was unanimously elected.

On motion of Mr. Wm. A. Little, Resolved that a Committee of three be appointed by the Mayor to take into consideration the recommendation of suitable persons to fill the Offices of the Corporation and to report to the next meeting of the Council.

The Mayor appointed Messrs. Wm. A. Little, Geo. W. Eve, & Peter Couse as the Committee under the foregoing resolution.

Ordered that when the Council adjourn, it adjourn to meet on Thursday next at eight o'clock P.M.

And the Council adjourned till Thursday next at 8 O'clock P.M.

[M. Slaughter, Mayor]

At an adjourned meeting of the Common Council of the Town of Fred[ericks]burg, held at the Council Chamber on Tuesday evening April 23rd 1868.

Present– M. Slaughter, Mayor

Wm. C. Morrison, D.C. Ellis, J.G. Hurkamp, C.E. Hunter, Wm. J. Jefferies, Geo. W. Eve.

Mr. L.A. Beardsley, appointed a member of the Council by Genl. Schofield, appeared, was qualified before the Mayor, by taking the Oath prescribed by the Act of Congress passed July 2nd 1862, and took his seat at the Board.

Present– L.C. Frost, Ab. P. Rowe, Wm. A. Little.

Mr. Wm. A. Little, Chairman of the Committee appointed at the last meeting of the Council, to recommend suitable persons to fill the various Offices of the Corporation, made [a] report in writing, accompanied by recommendations of the various persons mentioned in the report, which on motion of Mr. L.C. Frost was adopted–and laid on the table for the present.

And then the Council adjourned.

[M. Slaughter, Mayor]

At a called meeting of the Common Council of the Town of Fredericksb[ur]g held at the Council Chamber on Tuesday the 28th day of April 1868.

Present– M. Slaughter, Mayor
Geo. W. Eve, Peter Couse, L.A. Beardsley, Wm. J. Jefferies, Wm. H. Cunningham, Wm. A. Little, J.G. Hurkamp, Chas. E. Hunter, D.C. Ellis.

The Mayor stated that the Council had been convened for the purpose of receiving a communication from Lieut. G.G. Greenough, Military Commissioner, informing the Council of the appointment of Mr. Chas. E. Mallam as Mayor of the City of Fredericksburg and Mr. L.C. Frost as Recorder.

Mr. Chas. E. Mallam, appointed Mayor of the City of Fredericksburg under orders of Maj. Genl. Schofield, appeared, was qualified before M. Slaughter, Esqr. by taking the Oath prescribed by the Code of Virginia, & also the oath prescribed by the Act of Congress passed July 2nd 1868, and took his seat at the Board as Presiding Officer.

The following resolution offered by Mr. Wm. A. Little was unanimously adopted and ordered to spread on the minutes of the Council and published in the papers of the Town.

Resolved, that in parting with their late Presiding Officer & Mayor, M. Slaughter, who for the last eight years has occupied the position & performed so faithfully the duties of the said office, it is proper and becoming in us the members of the Common Council of Fredericksburg, to give expression to our united & unanimous opinion as to his satisfactory performance of said duties & to tender to him, as we do hereby, the assurances of our high appreciation of his said services, and of our cordial respect and esteem.

On motion of Mr. G.W. Eve, the report of the Committee on Officers of this Corporation was taken up—and the report was read by the Clerk of the Council.

On motion of Mr. Eve, Resolved that the Council will now proceed to recommend to Genl. Schofield a suitable person to be appointed a Police Officer for the [this] Corporation.

Mr. Eve nominated Chas. H. Wheeler for the office.

Mr. Hurkamp nominated P. Markey.

Mr. Little stated that all the persons mentioned in the report of the Committee were considered as candidates, except Geo. S. Green, who desired his name to be withdrawn.

Whereupon the vote was taken by ballot and resulted as follows, Viz:

For P. Markey   6 votes
" Chas. H. Wheeler   2 "
" W.C. Smith   1 "

L.P. Markey was declared to be duly recommended.

The Council then proceeded to recommend a suitable person for Measurer of Coal & wood, the following persons being candidates, M. Montgomery, Jos. E. Lordly & Thos. L. Savage, & the vote being taken resulted as follows:

For M. Montgomery   5 votes
" Thos. E. Lordley   4 "

So Mr. Montgomery was declared to be duly elected [recommended].

For Clerk of the Market the following were in nomination

Jno. D. Elder, Wm. J. Jones & Jno. Mannix & the vote being taken by ballot, resulted as follows:

For Wm. J. Jones   6 votes
" Jno. D. Elder   4[3] "

So Wm. J. Jones was declared to be duly recommended.

On motion of Mr. Hurkamp, ordered that it be recommended to Genl. Schofield to retain the present Board of Overseers of the Poor.

On motion of Mr. Eve, Ordered that it be recommended to Genl. Schofield to retain Mr. [W.] Hart, the present incumbent, as Commissioner of the Revenue for this Corporation.

Present– Ab. P. Rowe

On motion of Mr. Hurkamp, ordered that the report of the Committee on Officers, in regard to the Office of Clerk of the Council & Chamberlain of the Corporation be adopted, that it be recommended that the present incumbent be retained in Office.

On motion of Mr. Hurkamp, ordered that it be recommended to Genl. Schofield to retain the present incumbent, L.J. Huffman, as collector of taxes for this Corporation, there being no other eligible person [offering], who can qualify.

Mr. Wm. H. Cunningham, Chairman of the Gas Committee, submitted a report in writing, which on motion of Mr. Hurkamp was received.

After some remarks from Mr. Bradley & Mr. Sener, who were heard by permission of the Council, the following resolution offered by Mr. Hurkapmp was adopted,

Resolved that the Corporation will commence to use Gas in the Streets of the Town on the 1st day of May 1868, and that the Chamberlain be empowered to sign the books of the Gas Company.

On motion of Mr. Little, Resolved that the present Committee on Gas be requested to ascertain what arrangement can be made for lighting & extinguishing the lamps & to report that and also any other information on the subject.

Resolved, that when the Council adjourn, it adjourn to meet again on tomorrow night at 8 O'clock.

And then the Council adjourned.

[Chas. E. Mallam, Mayor]

At an adjourned meeting of the [Common] Council of the Town of Fredericksburg held at the Council Chamber on Wednesday [evening] the 29th day of April 1868.

Present– Chas. E. Mallam, Mayor

Wm. A. Little, Geo. W. Eve, Jno. G. Hurkamp, Wm. H. Cunningham, Chas. E. Hunter, Wm. H. Cunningham (sic), Wm. J. Jefferies, W.C. Morrison, L. A. Beardsley, D.C. Ellis, L.C. Frost.

Mr. L.C. Frost, appointed by order[s] from Genl. Schofield, Recorder of this Corporation, was qualified before Chas. E. Mallam, Mayor, by taking the oath prescribed by the State of Virginia and by the United States.

Present– Peter Couse.

Mr. Wm. H. Cunningham, Chairman of the Gas Committee, submitted a verbal report as to lighting and extinguishing the Gas lamps and also the proposition in writing of Mr. Wm.G. Hancock to light & extinguish the lamps.

On motion of Mr. Wm. A. Little, Resolved that the night Watch be dispensed with from and after the 1st day of May 1868.

The Mayor read the application of Wm. White to be appointed as lamp lighter.

Mr. Wm. H. King was also nominated.

Mr. Thos. Sullivan was also nominated.

On motion of Mr. Eve, Resolved that the compensation for lighting & extinguishing the lamps in the Streets of the Town, be fixed at the rate of two hundred Dollars per annum & shall not at any time exceed that rate [amount].

The vote being taken by ballot, Mr. Wm. G. Hancock was unanimously appointed to light and extinguish the Gas lamps.

The Mayor read a communication from S. Richardson which on motion of Mr. Little was laid on the table.

The Mayor also read a communication from Mr. W. Wallace Davis, and on motion of Mr. Little, the Clerk of the Council was directed to furnish to Mr. Davis the required information.

The Mayor appointed the following standing Committees, Viz:
On Finance–Wm. A. Little, Wm. H. Cunningham, L.C. Frost.
On Public Property–J.G. Hurkamp, Geo. W. Eve, W.C. Morrison.
On Streets–D.C. Ellis, Chas. E. Hunter, & Wm. J. Jefferies.
On Pump–Ab. P. Rowe, L.A. Beardsley, & Peter Couse.

On motion of Mr. Little, ordered that the vote ruling [fixing] the salary of Superintendent of Streets be paid at One Hundred dollars per annum [at two hundred dollars be reconsidered].

[On motion of Mr. Hurkamp, Ordered that the salary of the Superintendent of Streets be fixed at One Hundred dollars per annum.]

On motion of Mr. Eve, Ordered that the Police Officers be directed to have One hundred & fifty hand bills struck off and posted about the Town, notifying the Citizens that on and after the 10th day of May next, the ordinance in regard to Hogs going at large will be strictly enforced.

And then the Council adjourned.
[Chas. E. Mallam, Mayor]

At a called meeting of the Common Council of the Town of Fredericksburg held at the Council Chamber on Tuesday evening the 5th day of May 1868.

Present– Chas. E. Mallam, Mayor
Wm. A. Little, J.G. Hurkamp, Geo. W. Eve, Wm. J. Jefferies, Peter Couse, Ab. P. Rowe, Chas. E. Hunter, L.A. Beardsley, Wm. H. Cunningham, Wm. C. Morrison.

Fredericksburg's original clock mechanism had arms extending to the multiple clock faces in the steeple of St. George's Church, which kept them showing the same time. This mechanical system was replaced by electric works in the 1990s.

The Mayor stated the Council had been convened at the instance of the [Chairman of the] Pub. Prop. Committee who desired to make a statement to the Council.

The Chairman of the said Committee, Mr. Hurkamp, stated that on yesterday an offer was made to purchase the Fair Grounds for the sum of Twenty five hundred dollars in currency and that the Council had been convened for the purpose of laying the offer before them for acceptance or rejection, but [that] the gentleman who made the offer declined this evening to sign a written offer to the Council & intimated that he desired to consider the matter further.[13]

On motion of Mr. Cunningham–

Resolved, that the Publ[ic] Prop[erty] Committee be instructed to sell the property known as the "Fair Grounds" for a sum not less than twenty five hundred dollars, the proceeds to be converted under the direction of the Finance Committee, into the Bonds of the Corporation on the most favorable terms possible.

Present– D.C. Ellis

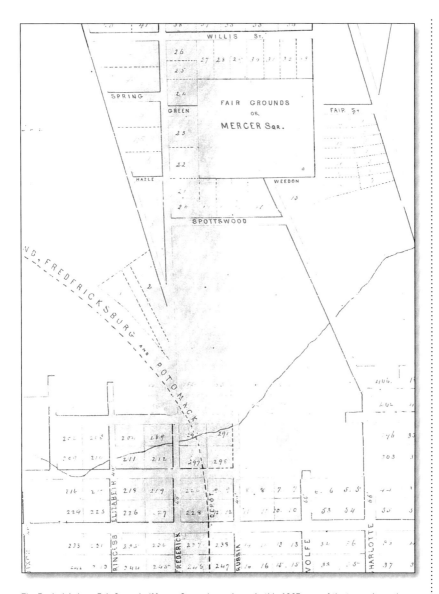

The Fredericksburg Fair Grounds (Mercer Square) are shown in this 1867 map of the town, drawn by Corporation Surveyor Carter M. Braxton.

L.C. Frost, Recorder

On motion of Mr. Eve, Ordered that Mr. Wm. J. Moon procure from the Committee, appointed to superintend the repairs to the Town Clock, a certificate that the work has been done according to the contract and for the price contracted [for.] And that upon [the] production of [the] said certificate & the refunding bond the Chamberlain be directed to pay the amount of his bill to Mr. Moon.

The Mayor stated that a notice had been served on him by T.S. Coleman to recover two years interest on certain bonds of the Corporation held by him, whereupon it was moved and seconded that the Pub[lic] Prop[erty] Committee be empowered to employ council [counsel] to defend the interests of the Corporation in the said suit, And the motion was adopted.

Mr. Jas. Hayes, Prest. of the Board of Overseers of the Poor, by note in writing, resigned his position, which was on motion accepted.

Mr. Thomas Griffin was unanimously appointed a member of the Board of Overseers of the Poor, to supply the vacancy occasioned by the resignation of Mr. Jas. Hayes.

On motion of Mr. Eve, Ordered that the Finance Committee be requested to ascertain the amount of the entire indebtedness of the Corporation and also & also (sic) of the assets of the Corporation, and report the same to the next meeting of the Council.

The Mayor read a communication from Geo. H. Peyton & sundry others, complaining of the present system of licenses for selling liquor to be drank where sold and asking relief from the same, which on motion was laid on the table for the present.

And then the Council adjourned.

[Chas. E. Mallam, Mayor]

At a meeting of the Common Council of the Town of Fredericksburg held at the Council Chamber on Saturday evening May 23rd 1868.

Present– Chas. E. Mallam, Mayor

L.C. Frost, Recorder

Wm. J. Jefferies, Wm. A. Little, L.A. Beardsley, Chas. E. Hunter, D.C. Ellis, J.G. Hurkamp, Wm. C. Morrison.

The Mayor presented a communication from Maj. Genl. Schofield in regard to some omission in the recommendation of persons to fill the

Offices of the Corporation.

On motion, Ordered that it be recommended to Maj. Genl. Schofield to retain Chas. E. Bragden in office as Measurer of Wood, Lumber &c, there being no other applicant for the office.

On motion, Ordered that it be recommended to Maj. Genl. Schofield to retain Carter M. Braxton in office as Surveyor of the Corporation, there being no other applicant for the office.

On motion of Mr. Little, Ordered that the Mayor be authorized to send Nelson Saunders, a colored lunatic, to the City of Richmond, where he can be properly cared for, and to draw upon the Chamberlain for the expenses of the removal.

The Finance Committee through its Chairman Mr. Little, made a report in writing and also an ordinance imposing taxes for the year 1868, which report on motion was adopted.

The Ordinance imposing taxes for the year 1868 recommended by the Finance Committee was passed and is in the words and figures following, to wit:

Be it ordained by the Mayor & Common Council of the Corporation of Fred[erick]sburg. that there shall be levied and Collected upon the persons & subjects liable to taxation [with]in said Corporation, for the year ending the 3rd Monday in March, 1869, the following taxes, to wit:

On Real Estate $1.25 on the $100 value.

On Personal Property $1.25 on the $100 value.

On every male person over the age of twenty one years, three dollars.

On licenses on [to] all persons required to be licensed by the State laws of Virginia within the said Corporation, except Brokers & Real Estate Agents, a license [tax] of three fourths of the State License imposed for the current year.

On Incomes, interest & salaries and all other subjects of State taxation, within the Corporation, three fourths of the State tax for the current year.

On licenses to Real Estate Agents & Brokers 50 per cent of the State tax for the current year.

Of which tax the Collector shall be authorized to receive one third in money and two thirds in the Corporation interest or past due obligations of the Corporation.[14]

A deduction of five per cent shall be allowed [up]on all taxes paid to the Collector on or before the 15th day of August 1868, and of three per cent of all taxes paid to the Collector on or before the 15th day of September 1868, and said taxes shall be liable to be distrained for on and after the 1st day of October 1868.

Be it ordained by the Mayor & Common Council of the Town of Fredericksburg, that a tax be levied and collected on all male dogs of $1.25 and on all female dogs of $2.25 for the year ending third Monday in March 1869 – this ordinance to take effect on and after the 10th day of June 1868.

Ordered that the Police Officers be directed to give notice immediately of the foregoing ordinance by posting hand bills throughout the town.

On motion, Ordered that the Mayor be authorized to contract for the purchase of as many collars & medals as may be necessary to supply the owners of dogs, provided the price shall not exceed twenty five cents each.

And then the Council adjourned.

[Chas. E. Mallam, Mayor]

At a regular meeting of the Common Council of the Town of Fredericksburg held at the Council Chamber [on] Tuesday Evening the 23rd day of June 1868.

Present– Chas. E. Mallam, Mayor

L.C. Frost, Recorder

Wm. A. Little, Geo. W. Eve, Peter Couse, Wm. H. Cunningham, Wm. J. Jefferies, Chas. E. Hunter, Ab. P. Rowe, Wm. C. Morrison.

The Mayor reported that he had received the Commissions of M. Montgomery as Measurer of Coal, grain, salt &c., and Wm. J. Jones as Clerk of the Market and that they had taken the necessary oaths before him & entered on the discharge of the duties of their offices.

The Mayor [also] stated that he had received the Commission of P. Markey as Police Officer, but that Mr. Markey declined now to take the Oath required under the act of Congress on July 2nd 1862.

On motion of Mr. Eve, Ordered that Chas. W. Edrington be appointed a Police Officer for the Corporation temporarily until the Mayor can recommend some suitable person to fill the Office who can qualify readily [regularly] under the existing laws of the United States.

The Mayor also presented a communication from Thomas Branch & Co. which on motion was referred to the Finance Committee for action and report.

The Mayor also stated to the Council that he had to day, in company with the Superintendent of Streets, inspected the Streets of the Town and found many nuisances existing, whereupon On motion of Mr. Little,

Resolved, that the Mayor be and he is hereby requested to enforce strictly hereafter the provisions of the Corporation ordinances prohibiting the deposit of filth, ashes &c in the Streets & footways of the Town.

On motion of Mr. Little, Resolved, that the Pub[lic] Prop[erty] Committee be and they are hereby instructed to cause the District Court Room & the iron railing & gates to the Court House lot to be repaired.

On motion, ordered that Mr. A.P. Rowe be authorized to clean out the Market House lot on the same terms as last year—commencing the 1st of July next, for the space of one year.

And then the Council adjourned.

[Chas. E. Mallam, Mayor]

At a called meeting of the Common Council of the Town of Fredericksburg held at the Council Chamber on Thursday evening July 30th 1868.

Present– Chas. E. Mallam, Mayor
L.C. Frost, Recorder

Geo. W. Eve, Jno. G. Hurkamp, Wm. H. Cunningham, Wm. J. Jefferies, Ab. P. Rowe, Peter Couse.

The Mayor presented a communication from Lewis L. Layton proposing to remove two wrecks now obstructing the Channel of the River opposite of the Wharves, which on motion of Mr. Hurkamp was referred to the Street Committee for examination & report to the next meeting of the Council.

The Mayor presented a communication from Robt. Stairs offering himself as a candidate for Police Officer, which on motion was laid on the table.

The Mayor presented a communication from Mr. G.A. Myers on behalf of Messrs. Hoyer & Ludwig in regard to a claim against the Corporation for lithographing small notes in the year 1861, which on motion was referred to the Finance Committee for investigation & report.

On motion of Mr. Frost, Resolved that the Chamberlain be authorized to borrow a sum not exceeding Four Hundred Dollars from the fund arising from the sale of the Fair Grounds, to be appropriated to cleaning the

Streets and gutters of the town, the said sum of Four Hundred Dollars to be returned to the said fund out of the first taxes that may be received.

A bill of C.W. Edrington against the Corporation for going to Stafford, by order of Jno. Coakley, acting Coroner, amounting to $4.00 was ordered to be paid.

[A bill of J.S.G. Timberlake for summoning coroner's jury & burying dead body amounting to $4.00 was ordered to be paid.]

Mr. Wm. H. Cunningham, for [from] the Gas Committee, returned to the Council a list of all the persons who subscribed to the erection of the lamp posts, lamps &c & [a] report showing the receipts & expenditures of the Gas Committee, leaving a balance in the hands of the Council [Committee] of $105.64, and asked that a new Committee on Gas be appointed, which report was received and ordered to be filed.

The Mayor [appointed] as the Gas Committee Messrs. Hurkamp, Cunningham & Hunter.

On motion of Mr. Hurkamp, Ordered that notice be given immediately by hand bills posted about the town that on and after the 10th day of August next, all dogs belonging to the residents of the town found running at large in the Streets of the town, without a collar such as is prescribed by the ordinance[s] of the Corporation, shall be liable to be caught & confined for twenty four hours. The owner of a dog so caught can redeem him by paying a fine of two dollars for each time his or her dog may be caught, One half going [to go] to the Officer catching the dog & the other half to the Corporation. At the expiration of twenty four hours if not redeemed, said dog[s] will be killed.

Ordered that the Chamberlain be instructed to renew two lost registered bonds of the Corporation for $100 [each] to Mrs. Mary G. Henderson, who [she] having advertised the same according to law—and give the usual indemnifying bond.

And then the Council adjourned.

[Chas. E. Mallam, Mayor]

At a [called] meeting of the Common Council of the Town of Fredericksburg held at the Council on Monday Evening the 31st day of August, 1868.

Present– C.E. Mallam, Mayor
L.C. Frost, Recorder
L.A. Beardsley, Chas. E. Hunter, Peter Couse, Geo. W. Eve, Wm. H. Cunningham, Wm. J. Jefferies, Ab. P. Rowe, D.C. Ellis.

It appearing to the Council that the Mayor & Chamberlain have executed their individual bonds, the one as original & the other as security, in the penalty of five hundred dollars, which bond was rendered necessary in order to obtain a [writ of] supersedeas to [a] judgment of the Circuit Court of Spotsylvania County in favor of Thomas S. Coleman against the Mayor & Chamberlain of Fredericksburg the Council doth sanction the execution of [the] said bond & doth hereby pledge the faith of the Corporation to the indemnity of the said Mayor & Chamberlain.

It appearing to the Council that certain holders of the bonds of the Corporation of the denomination of One hundred Dollars & under, are desirous to consolidate their bonds into larger bonds, it is hereby ordered that the Finance Committee be and they are hereby ordered [authorized] whenever in their judgment the interest[s] of the Corporation will not be thereby impaired, to instruct the Chamberlain to consolidate the small bonds of the Corporation into larger ones upon the application of the holders, the said small bonds to be cancelled by the Chamberlain and destroyed by the Finance Committee at the annual settlement in March.

Mr. Geo. W. Eve moved that the sum of fifty dollars be appropriated for the purpose of building a Music Stand on the Public Square for the use of the Band, which motion was rejected.

Mr. Cunningham presented a communication from Mr. Elzay Payne in regard to a fine imposed upon him by the Mayor for driving a dray in the Streets of the Town without a license, and on motion—Mr. St. Geo. R. Fitzhugh was heard on the subject, when on the motion of Mr. Eve the matter was indefinitely postponed.

The Mayor stated that he had been requested to mention to the Council that a vane was at the service of the Council, provided that it should be put up on the Court House, when Mr. Rowe moved that a sum not exceeding thirty dollars be appropriated for the purpose of putting up the vane, but

The weather vane atop the court house cupola, the subject of discussion on August 31, 1868, is still in place.

afterwards withdrew the motion: When Mr. Frost moved that the Pub[lic] Property Committee be authorized to expend the sum of twenty dollars, in addition to the repairs necessary for the roof of the Court House, in putting up the vane, which motion, after a division, was adopted.

The Street Committee made a verbal report in regard to the removal of the wrecks in the river, when on motion of Mr. Frost, the said Street Committee were authorized to proceed at once to have the said wreck removed in the most economical manner.

It appearing to the Council that the Commissioner of the Revenue has not as yet furnished to the Collector of taxes his books for the current year, On motion of Mr. Eve the Recorder, Mr. Frost, was requested to call on the Commissioner and ascertain his reasons for the delay & to report to the Council at an adjourned meeting of the Council to be held on Tuesday evening the 8th proximo.

And then the Council adjourned till Tuesday the 8th prox.

[Chas. E. Mallam, Mayor]

At an adjourned meeting of the Common Council of the Town of Fredericksburg held at the Council Chamber on Tuesday the 8th day of September 1868.

Present– Chas. E. Mallam, Mayor
L.C. Frost, Recorder
Wm. J. Jefferies, Chas. E. Hunter, Peter Couse, D.C. Ellis, Geo. W. Eve, J.G. Hurkamp.

Mr. Frost stated that in obedience to instructions of the Council he had called on Mr. Hart, the Commissioner of the Revenue, to ascertain his reasons for not having his books ready for the Collector of taxes, that the Comnr. informed him that he had been prevented from completing his books on account of sickness and assured him that he would have the books ready certainly by the 1st day of October next—which report on motion of Mr. Eve was received.

On motion of Mr. Hurkamp, Ordered that a discount of five per cent be allowed to all persons who shall pay their taxes on or before the 15th day of October, and a discount of three per cent to all who shall pay their taxes on or before the 15th day of November 1868.

Present– Wm. H. Cunningham

The Mayor presented a communication from C.E. Bragden, Harbor Master, calling the attention of the Council to the condition of the Wharf at the foot of Dixon Street, belonging to Dr. M.A. Blankman, a non resident of this State and on motion of Mr. Frost, Ordered that the Clerk of the Council be instructed to enclose a copy of the communication of Mr. Bragden to Dr. Blankman at Washington City, and to notify him that the said Wharf must be properly repaired within thirty days, and if not so repaired the Council will take further action on the matter.

And then the Council adjourned.
[Chas. E. Mallam, Mayor]

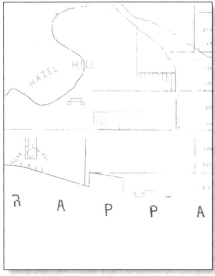

Detail from an 1867 map of Fredericksburg showing the town wharves, drawn by Corporation Surveyor Carter M. Braxton.

At a called meeting of the Common Council held at the Council Chamber on Tuesday evening Sept. 29th 1868.

Present– Chas. E. Mallam, Mayor
L.C. Frost, Recorder

Geo. W. Eve, L.A. Beardsley, Peter Couse, Wm. H. Cunningham, J.G. Hurkamp, Chas. E. Hunter, Wm. J. Jefferies, Ab. P. Rowe, D.C. Ellis.

The Mayor having reported that the Police Officers had discharged their duties satisfactorily for the quarter ending the 16th inst., Ordered that the Chamberlain pay them their salaries up to that time.

And then the Council adjourned.

[Chas. E. Mallam, Mayor]

At a called meeting of the Common Council of the Town of Fredericksburg held at the Council Chamber on Saturday evening the 10th of October 1868.

Present– Chas. E. Mallam, Mayor
L.C. Frost, Recorder

Wm. H. Cunningham, Chas. E. Hunter, Geo. W. Eve, J.G. Hurkamp, Wm. J. Jefferies, Peter Couse.

The Mayor stated that the Council had been convened for the purpose of considering the propriety of sending delegates to an adjourned meeting of the Bristol Convention to be held in the City of Norfolk on the 14th inst. to consider the Rail Road interests of the South & the establishment of direct trade with Europe, when on the motion of Mr. Hurkamp,

Resolved that the Mayor be authorized to appoint twenty five or more delegates to attend the said Convention and that the Mayor's name be added to the list.[15]

And then the Council adjourned.

[Chas. E. Mallam, Mayor]

At a meeting of the Common Council of the Town of Fredericksburg held at the Council Chamber on Tuesday the 24th day of November 1868.

Present– Chas. E. Mallam, Mayor

Geo. W. Eve, Ab. P. Rowe, Wm. A. Little, Peter Couse, C.E.Hunter, J.G.

Hurkamp, Wm. H. Cunningham.

Ordered that a bill of Waite & Sener's, amounting to the sum of $26.00, which is allowed by the Council, be paid by the Chamberlain.

On motion ordered that Mr. Jas. Mazeen be permitted to erect a privy in the Market House lot, on condition that the same be kept clean and in good order, for the use of parties who rent stalls in the Market & that said privy be located under the directions of the Public Property Committee.

On motion of Mr. Hunter, Ordered that Section 1 of Chapter V of the ordinances be amended in this, that the words "or by railroads" be inserted after the word basin, in the fourth line of said ordinance and in the first section.

And then the Council adjourned.

[Chas. E. Mallam, Mayor]

At a regular meeting of the Common Council of the Town of Fredericksburg held at the Council Chamber, on Tuesday evening the 22nd day of Decr. 1868.

Present– Chas. E. Mallam, Mayor
Wm. A. Little, L.A. Beardsley, Jno. G. Hurkamp, Wm. J. Jefferies, Wm. C. Morrison, Geo. W. Eve, D.C. Ellis, Chas. E. Hunter.

The Mayor presented a copy of an order passed at the December term of the Corporation Court in regard to the uncomfortable condition of the present Court room, which was read by the Clerk of the Council, when on motion of Mr. Little, Resolved that it be recommended to the Corporation Court, to make use of the District Court Room for the sessions of the said Court, during the said [winter]months.

The Mayor having reported favorably, Ordered that the Chamberlain pay the Police Officers their salaries for the quarter ending on the 16th inst.

Present– Peter Couse

On motion of Mr. Little, ordered that Mr. J.G. Hurkamp be requested to ascertain upon what terms he can purchase One thousand feet of serviceable hose, either new or second hand, to be used with the Corporation Fire Engine and report at the next meeting of the Council.

On motion of Mr. Little, ordered that Mr. J.G. Hurkamp be requested to ascertain upon what terms he can purchase one thousand feet of serviceable hose. (sic, this line is a repeat)

On motion of Mr. Little, ordered that the Clerk of the Council be directed to prepare at once a copy of the Communication addressed to the Council by C.E. Bragden, Harbor Master, in regard to Dr. Blankman's Wharf and also of the resolution passed by the Council on the 8th day of September, 1868, in regard thereto and cause the same to be properly served on Mr. C.W. Wallace, the Attorney of Dr. [M.A.] Blankman.

The following offered by Mr. Little was unanimously adopted—

Resolved, that all laws in respect to crimes & punishment & to criminal proceedings applicable to White persons in the By Laws of the [this] Corporation, shall apply in like manner to colored persons, and that all laws inconsistent with this provision be and they are hereby repealed.

And then the Council adjourned.

[Chas. E. Mallam, Mayor]

—— 1869 ——

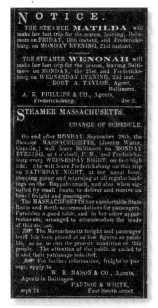

Steamer schedule from the January 21, 1869 issue of the Virginia Herald, which was published in Fredericksburg.

At a meeting of the Common Council of the Town of Fredericksburg held at the Council Chamber on Tuesday evening the 26th day of Jan[uar]y 1869.

Present– Chas. E. Mallam, Mayor

L.C. Frost, Recorder

Messrs. Wm. A. Little, L.A. Beardsley, Wm. C. Morrison, Wm. J. Jefferies, Jno. G. Hurkamp, Geo. W. Eve, D.C. Ellis & Ab.P. Rowe.

The Mayor presented a proposition from Mr. J.B. Ficklen, tendering the sum of $1500 in currency for the interest of the Corporation in the house on Main Street in which he now holds an interest dependent on one life– And on motion of Mr. Little, Resolved that the fee simple title to the said property be offered to Mr. Ficklen for the sum of $6500 in the bonds of the Corporation, provided the said offer accepted within thirty days.

The Mayor also presented a communication from Messrs. M. Eldridge & Co. through Mr. J.E.

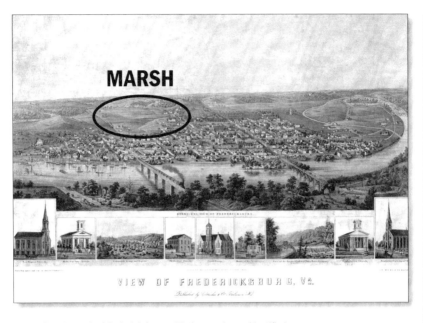

An 1850s lithograph of Fredericksburg, with the marsh area identified.

Tackett, Agents of the Alexa. & New York & Alexa. & Philada. Steam lines, asking the Cooperation of the Common Council in establishing a permanent Steam communication via Aquia Creek, from Fredericksburg to New York & Philadelphia and on motion
—Mr. Jno. E. Tackett & Mr. J. Newton Harper were heard on the subject–
When on motion of Mr. Little, Resolved, that a committee of four members of the Council be appointed by the Mayor to confer with the Committee of the Board of Trade & also with the Committee of the said Steam Boat Company, on the subject presented in the above communication.

The Mayor appointed as the Committee under the foregoing resolution Messrs. L.C. Frost, J.G. Hurkamp, D.C. Ellis & Wm. A. Little.

On motion of Mr. J.G. Hurkamp, Resolved that Mr. Jno. E. Tackett be added to the above committee.

Mr. Jno. E. Tackett, by permission of the Council, called the attention of the Council to the condition of the Marsh in the western suburbs of the Town, and on motion Mr. Geo. Aler was also heard on the same subject, when on motion of Mr. Little, Resolved that the whole subject be referred to the Street Committee, who are requested, with the assistance of the City

A post-war photo of the drainage ditch that was the subject of considerable discussion by the Fredericksburg Town Council.

Surveyor, to ascertain what is necessary to be done in the premises and what will be the probable costs thereof, and they are requested to make the necessary examination thereof as early as possible in order to report to a meeting of the Council, which will be called to receive their report.

A communication from Mr. Jno. M. Herndon was read and on motion the same was referred to the Finance Committee for investigation and report.

A bill of Scott & Bowering amounting to the sum of Eleven dollars & fifty cents for adjusting the Bell of the Town Clock was allowed and ordered to be paid.

[A bill of Johnston & Co. amounting to $10.51 was allowed & ordered to be paid.]

An account of Dr. B.S. Herndon was read and on motion referred to the Finance Committee for investigation and report to the next meeting of the Council.

Mr. Hurkamp who was appointed at the last meeting of the Council to ascertain the cost of Hose &c, made a verbal report, and on motion Mr. Bowering was heard on the subject, and after some discussion, on motion of Mr. Frost, Resolved, that a committee of four be appointed by the Mayor to ascertain and report to the next meeting of the Council any feasible plan for furnishing [a] suitable fire apparatus for the town—and also any information they can obtain in regard to the cost of a Steam Fire Engine or other apparatus or plan which will furnish the best protection to the town from fire.

A bill of Wm. A. Little amounting to the sum of Seventy five dollars was allowed and ordered to be paid.

The Mayor appointed as the Committee on a Fire Apparatus, Messrs. Frost, Hunter, Morrison & Hurkamp.

[Chas. E. Mallam, Mayor]

At a meeting of the Common Council of the Town of Fredericksburg held at the Council Chamber on Tuesday evening the 23rd day of February 1869.

Present– Chas. E. Mallam, Mayor
        L.C. Frost, Recorder
Messrs. Wm. A. Little, Geo. W. Eve, L.A. Beardsley, Wm. J. Jefferies, Jno. G. Hurkamp, Wm. H. Cunningham, Peter Couse, Chas. E. Hunter.

The Special Committee on a Fire Apparatus requested time until the next meeting of the Council in order to make a full and final report, which on motion of Mr. Cunningham was granted.

The Mayor presented a plat and survey of lot, formerly Betty Minor's, which was sold for taxes in to Mr. Thomas Manuel—and it appearing to the Council that the said plat and survey is made out by the Corporation Surveyor, in accordance with Section 7, Chapter 40 of the Ordinance of the Corporation—on motion of Mr. Little the same is ordered to be recorded.

Present– D.C. Ellis

It being announced that a committee from the Young Men's Christian Association were in attendance, on motion of Mr. Eve, & by consent of the Council Mr. St. Geo. R. Fitzhugh made a statement on behalf of the Association asking that a room be appropriated by the Council for the use of the Association, When on motion of Mr. Frost, Resolved that the Young Men's Christian Association be allowed the choice of two rooms, the one on the left and the other on the right, of the present Council Chamber, to be occupied during the pleasure of the Council for the uses and purposes of the Association.

Mr. D.C. Ellis, Chairman of the Street Committee, made a verbal report in regard to the condition of the Kenmore Marsh, and the Mayor also presented a written report in regard to the matter from C.M. Braxton, Corporation Surveyor, & also the written offers of several persons, owners of the lands lying adjacent, to contribute [to] the proper drainage of the Marsh, When by consent of the Council Mr. Braxton made some remarks on the subject, When Mr. Frost moved that the sum of $250., be appropriated to draining the said Marsh, to be expended under the superintendence of the Corporation Surveyor, & in conjunction with the offers of individuals referred to above & also the tenders of Messrs. Hurkamp, Rowe & Hoomes, to which motion Mr. Eve offered as an amendment that the whole matter be recommitted to the Street Committee for further report— which amendment was lost, and the question recurring on the motion of Mr. Frost it was adopted.

An account of J.H. Kelly amounting to $19.00 was allowed and ordered to be paid.

And then the Council adjourned.

[Chas. E. Mallam, Mayor]

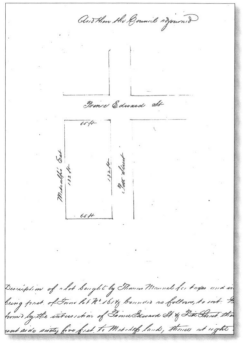

This sketch from the original Council minutes shows the property at 1417-1419 Prince Edward Street, which has since been subdivided and re-platted.

Description of a lot bought by Thomas Manuel for taxes and in part of Thos. F. Knox, the same being part of Town lot No. 161 & bounded as follows, to wit: Beginning at the northwest corner formed by the intersection of Prince Edward St. & Pitt Street, thence with Prince Edward St. on the west side sixty five feet to Metcalf land, thence at right angles to said Prince Edward St. and parallel to Pitt St. one hundred & thirty two feet, thence at right angles to last line & parallel to Prince Edward Street sixty five feet to Pitt St., thence one hundred & thirty two feet, along the north side of Pitt St. to the point of beginning.

Carter M. Braxton, Corporation Surveyor
    Feby. 22nd, 1869

 The above plat & survey was examined by the Council at a meeting held on the 23rd day of February 1869 & ordered to be recorded.
    Teste R.S. Chew, Clerk Council

At a called meeting of the Common Council held at the Council Chamber on Thursday the 1st day of April 1869.
 Present– Chas. E. Mallam, Mayor
    L.C. Frost, Recorder
Geo. W. Eve, Wm. J. Jefferies, D.C. Ellis, L.A. Beardsley, Peter Couse, Chas. E. Hunter.

 On motion R.S. Chew was appointed Clerk Pro Tempore.

 Wm. E. Straight appointed Clerk of the Council & Chamberlain of the Corporation appeared and was qualified before the Mayor, by taking the oath of Office & the Oath prescribed by the Act of Assembly passed July 2nd 1862.

 The Official Bond of Wm. E. Straight, Chamberlain of this Corporation, in the penalty of Ten thousand Dollars, with A.C. Underhill, D.W. Bailey & C.L. Straight as his securities was presented to the Council, approved and ordered to be delivered to the Mayor, to be by him deposited in the National Bank of Fredericksburg for safe keeping.

 L.E. Chaffee, appointed Collector of taxes for the Corporation, appeared and was qualified before the Mayor, by taking the Oaths of Office & the Oath prescribed by the Act of Congress passed July 2nd, 1862.

 The Official Bond of L.E. Chaffee, Collector of taxes for this Corporation, in the penalty of ten thousand Dollars, with Wm. Lang[er], G.W. Eve, Chas. E. Hunter & L.C. Frost as his securities, was presented to the Council, approved and ordered to be delivered to the Mayor, to be by him deposited in the National Bank of Fredericksburg for safe keeping.

 Messrs. F. Bauman & Henry Miller, appointed members of the Council, appeared and was [were] qualified before the Mayor, by taking the Oath[s] of Office & the Oath prescribed by the Act of Congress passed July 2nd, 1862 & took their seats at the Board.

 Morris Montgomery appointed Measurer of wood & Lumber appeared & was qualified before the Mayor by taking the oath of office & the oath prescribed by the Act of Congress passed July 2nd 1862.

On motion ordered that the late Clerk of the Council be directed to turn over all books & papers in his hands belonging to the Council to Wm. E. Straight the present Clerk of the Council.

On motion ordered that the late Chamberlain of the Corporation be directed to turn over all books, papers & monies in his hands belonging to the Corporation, to Wm. E. Straight the present Chamberlain.

On motion, ordered that the Finance Committee be directed to examine the accounts of the late Chamberlain & Collector of taxes & to make a report to the next meeting of the Council.

Ordered that the number of Police Officers be fixed at two, and thereupon the Council proceeded to ballot for them, Chas. W. Edrington, Wm. Way & Washington Jennings being in nomination, which resulted in the election of Chas. W. Edrington & Wm. Way as temporary Police Officers.

Absent– Chas. E. Mallam, Mayor

On motion the salary of the Mayor for the year ending the 3rd Monday in March 1870 was fixed at four hundred dollars.

Present– Chas. E. Mallam, Mayor

Mr. Hunter moved that the salary of the Police Officers be fixed at the sum of three hundred & fifty dollars, which motion after a division was lost.

Mr. Frost moved that the salary of the Police Officers be fixed at the sum of three hundred Dollars, which motion, after a division, was lost.

On motion of Mr. Eve, the salaries of all the Officers of the Council was (sic) fixed at the same [sum] as heretofore.

The Mayor appointed the following Committees–

    Finance Committee

L.C. Frost, Chas. E. Hunter, & Wm. C. Morrison

    Public Property

George W. Eve, Wm. J. Jefferies, Wm. C. Morrison

    Streets

L.C. Frost, Chas. E. Hunter, F. Bauman

    Pumps

Peter Couse, L.A. Beardsley, Henry Miller

Petition was presented by Chas. E. Hunter to allow Messrs. A.G. & C.G. Helper [Hepler] to close Frederick Street the depth of their property [to be opened] at any time by the order of the Council.

Petition granted.

On motion of Mr. Jefferies it was ordered that the license for drays and wagons be continued the same as the past year.

On motion of Mr. Frost, it was resolved that the Police Officers be given one half the fines imposed for violations of the laws of the Corporation.

On motion of Mr. Frost, it was resolved that Mr. Hurkamp be continued upon the Fire Com[mit]tee until the final report.

The Council then adjourned to meet at 7 O'clock on the 9th of April 1869.
    [W.E. Straight, Clerk
    Chas. E. Mallam, Mayor]

At an adjourned meeting of the Common Council held at the Council Chamber on Friday [the] 9th day of April 1869.

Present– Chas. E. Mallam, Mayor
    L.C. Frost, Recorder
Geo. W. Eve, Wm. J. Jefferies, Henry Miller, Wm. C. Morrison, Peter Couse, F. Bauman, W.C. Ellis, Chas. E. Hunter.

L.C. Frost asked and obtained leave, and did make a personal explanation. Mr. Frost then handed to the Mayor the resignation of himself, Mr. Chas. E. Hunter and W.C. Morrison to take effect when persons can be found and qualified to succeed them. On motion of Mr. Eve, their resignations were ordered to be laid on the table.

The Finance Committee through their Chairman Mr. Frost reported that they had examined the accounts of the late Chamberlain and find the same to be correct and a balance due him by the Corporation of $57.40, which amount they recommend to be refunded to him out of the first funds that may come into the hands of the [present] Chamberlain.

The Finance Committee through their Chairman Mr. Frost, reported that they had examined the accounts of L.J. Huffman late Collector of taxes and find the same to be correct & a balance of uncollected taxes in his hands amounting to the sum of $9,495.32.

The Mayor vacated the Chair to offer the following resolution which was accepted.

Resolved that the Council express its feelings of deep regret that circumstances have rendered it necessary that the accomplished Chamberlain & Clerk of the Council, Col. Robt. Chew, should vacate his office, it is felt by the [this] Body that the removal of Col. Chew will be a public loss. The manner in which he has conducted his responsible duties deserve the highest praise, therefore the thanks of the Council for his valuable services are hereby tendered to him, together with best wishes for his future prosperity.

The Finance Committee offered their report for the Current year, which was accepted and ordered to be recorded.

The Committee upon Fire Apparatus then offered their report, which was accepted.

The Mayor then presented the petition of Joseph Hall to close for the present Willis Street—Referred to the Street Committee.

The Mayor brought to the notice of the Council the unsafe condition of the Jail, Whereupon on motion of Mr. Frost, the matter was referred to the Committee on Public Property.

On motion of Mr. Hunter of the Finance Committee Mr. Heinichen on[e] of the Overseers of the Poor made an explanation in regard to the expenditures of the past year.

On motion of Mr. Frost, it was ordered that $1200 be appropriated to the maintenance of the Poor for the present year, under the superintendance (sic) of the same Overseers.

On Motion of Mr. Hunter, it was Ordered that the rations of Sugar & Coffee for the Poor be dispensed with except to the sick.

D.C. Ellis offered his resignation as a member of the Council and on motion of Mr. Eve it was accepted.

On motion of Mr. Hunter, it was ordered that the Collector be directed to collect at once the license for [from] all drays and wagons now due.

On Motion of Mr. Frost, it was ordered that the Pub[lic] Property Committee be hereby authorized to contract with some responsible party to wind up and keep in order the Public Clock for the current year, at a sum not exceeding $50.00.

On motion of Mr. Frost, it was ordered that the tax list be published in the Fredericksburg News.

Mr. Hunter gave notice that he would at the next meeting of the Council submit a motion that some grade be established for the streets of the Corporation.

On motion of Mr. Frost, it was ordered that the report of the Finance Committee for the fiscal year ending March 15th, 1869 be published in all three of the City papers.

The Council then adjourned.

[W.E. Straight, Clerk
Chas. E. Mallam, Mayor]

The Tax Bill reported by the Finance Committee for the year ending March 1870—

To the Mayor and Common Council of the City of Fredericksburg, The undersigned members of the Finance Committee, respectfully report that they have prepared and herewith submit an Ordinance imposing Taxes for the year ending the third Monday in March, 1870. They find that with the most economical administration of the affairs of the Corporation, it has required the sum of about Nine thousand ($9,000) dollars in money to meet necessary Municipal expenses, exclusive of the claims for interest on the Bonded debt of the City, which amount now to about thirteen thousand ($13,000) dollars annually. This current interest and some accumulation of interest past due were provided for in part by the Finance bill of the past year, by the City receiving two thirds of the taxes due her in interest Coupons. But as large amounts of Bonds are held out of this City, in various parts of the State, and even outside of the State, those Coupons are not annually sent in and bought by our tax payers, thereby leaving a considerable amount of [the] interest Coupons of the past year still unpaid. And one or more Bonds for raising wrecks, which will fall due in the current year, Your Comte. are therefore compelled to provide in the present tax bill for the payment of the interest for [of] the current year, and the above mentioned Bonds in money. At the same time your Committee realized the necessity of making the tax as light as possible and of receiving some portion of the tax of the current year also in coupons.

The Committee's Books shows the taxable subjects to be as follows:

Real Estate $1,282,838.00
Personal Property 120.000.00

Poll tax on 750 polls of which only about six hundred are available
Licenses in 1868, realized $6,539.72

Your Committee propose to levy the tax for the current year as follows:
On Real Estate $1.25 in the $100 value being same as last year
16,147.02
On Personal Property (also same as last year) $1.25 in the $100 value
4,678.12

On Persons $3.00 per head
   On Licenses, except Real Estate & Brokers, three fourths of the State tax for the current year
      6,539.72

      _____

      $27,364.86
Last Year $25,335.00

On incomes, interests and salaries and all other subjects of taxation in the Corporation three fourths of the State tax, and on licenses to Real Estate Agents and Brokers 50% [per cent] of the State tax for the current year,
On which your Committee recommend that one third be received in Coupons, interest and past due obligations, Viz:
      9,021.62
And two thirds be received in money, Viz:
      18,243.24

      _____

      $27,364.86

There remains due $9,495.32 of the last year taxes unpaid and in the hands of the Collector, from which your Committee believe a sufficient sum will be collected to make up any deficiency in the cash part of the taxes of the current year. Your Committee further recommends that a tax of One dollar per head upon all Male Dogs and two dollars upon all female Dogs, be imposed and that the Ordinance in regard to the tax collars for dogs as modified during the past summer by the present Council, be strictly enforced.

   We also recommend that the same deduction on taxes paid before the 15th of August & the 15th day September be made as last year.
         Respectfully submitted
         Signed L.C. Frost
         Chas. E. Hunter

At a regular meeting of the Common Council held at the Council Chamber Tuesday April 27th, 1869.
   Present– Chas. E. Mallam, Mayor
      L.C. Frost, Recorder

L.A. Beardsley, F. Bauman, Henry Miller, Wm. J. Jefferies, Geo. W. Eve, Wm. C. Morrison, Chas. E. Hunter.

Mr. T.B. Dunn, appointed Member of the Council appeared and declined to serve, giving as a reason that he had not the time to attend to the Meetings of the Council.

The Chairman of the Street Committee reported adversely to the granting of Mr. Hall's petition to close Willis Street, and on motion of Mr. Eve it was Resolved that the petition be not granted.

The Chairman of the Pub[lic] Property Committee, to whom the condition of the Jail was referred, reported that in their opinion that the Jail was now in as good and safe condition as it could be put in without its being [entirely] rebuilt.

But on motion of Mr. Frost, it was ordered that the lower cells be cased upon the inside with two inch Oak plank.

The Chairman of the Public Property Committee reported that he had made a contract with Mr. Murray to wind up and keep in order the Town Clock for the sum of $40 per annum and on motion the report was accepted.

Moved by C.E. Hunter that there shall be established by actual survey a standard grade for the streets and side walks of the City & that C.M. Braxton be and is hereby authorized to make said survey.

The resolution was carried by the following vote

Yeas– Beardsley, Bowman (sic), Hunter, Frost, Morrison, & Jefferies

Nay– Miller & Eve

The Mayor presented a bid from Chas. A. Grove offering to keep the City pumps in order for twelve months, and on Motion referred to the Pumps Committee.

On motion of Mr. Frost, it was ordered that the Chamberlain pay to the Captor of Albert Fortune the reward of Fifty dollars offered by the Mayor for his apprehension.

On motion of Mr. Frost, the Pumps Committee were requested to investigate and report at the next meeting on the condition of the Pump opposite the house of J.J. Chew, and to ascertain the best and cheapest method of obtaining water at that pump.

The Council then adjourned.

[Chas. E. Mallam, Mayor]

At a regular meeting of the Common Council held at the Council Chamber, Tuesday the 25th day of May 1869.

Present– Chas. E. Mallam, Mayor
           L.C. Frost, Recorder
Peter Couse, Henry Miller, F. Bowman (sic), Wm. J. Jefferies, Geo. W. Eve, Chas. E. Hunter.

On motion of Mr. Frost it was ordered that the bid of Mr. Grove for keeping the City pumps in order for the twelve months be laid on the table.

The Chairman of the Pumps Committee to whom was referred the condition of the City pump opposite Mr. Chews house reported that in their opinion the pump could not be repaired.

Present– W.C. Morrison.

On motion of L.C. Frost, resolved that the Pump Committee be and hereby is authorized to build one or two new wells and pumps in lien (sic) of those at Chews and Morrisons corners respectively without further report to this board.

Washington Jennings was nominated by the Mayor for appointment of Police Officer in place of Wm. Day, and on motion he was appointed to date from May 21st 1869.

On motion of Mr. Frost, Capt. G.S. Gunn was appointed a Police Officer for the City from this date.

On motion of Mr. Jefferies it was resolved that the Finance Committee insist on the Collector to destrain for any taxes now passed [past] due that are not paid at once.

On motion of Mr. Eve, it was resolved that the Mayor appoint a Committee of three to confer with himself in regard to the matter of imposing a special tax upon all Junk dealers—and that when this meeting adjourns to meet on Monday evening next to receive the report.

On motion of L.C. Frost, resolved that the board authorize and direct the Public Property Committee to furnish sufficient lumber to enclose two sides of the [public] burying grounds known as the Potters Field, provided the colored people do the labor of building said fence.

On motion of L.C. Frost, be resolved that so much of the Ordinance relating to dogs, which on the fourth line calls for a collar with a piece of metal attached thereto, be amended so as to read or leather strap to serve as a muzzle, the form of which shall be, arranged by the Mayor, to be paid for the same as the collars and metal and that said Collar and Muzzle be obtained from the Chamberlain.

The Council then adjourned to meet again on Monday evening next at 8 O'clock.

[W.E. Straight, Clerk
Chas. E. Mallam, Mayor]

At an adjourned meeting of the Common Council [held at the Council Chamber] the 31st day of May 1869.

Present– Chas. E. Mallam, Mayor
L.C. Frost, Recorder
F. Bowman (sic), Henry Miller, Peter Couse, Chas. E. Hunter, Wm. J. Morrison (sic), Geo. W. Eve, Wm. J. Jefferies, Geo. W. Eve (sic), [Chas. Miller].

The Committee appointed at the last meeting in the matter of imposing a special tax upon all Junk dealers, reported through their Chairman the Mayor, that they had prepared an Ordinance which they submit to the Council and after a considerable discussion the Ordinance was rejected.

On motion of Chas. E. Hunter, It was ordered that the Chamberlain is hereby authorized to issue a negotiable note for the payment of such sums as may be due to the Overseers of the Poor at this date.

V.E.I.

The Council then adjourned.
[W.E. Straight, Clerk
Chas. E. Mallam, Mayor]

At a regular meeting of the Common Council held at the Council Chamber the 22nd day of June 1869.

Present– Chas. E. Mallam, Mayor
Chas. Miller, F. Bowman (sic), Chas. E. Hunter, Henry Miller, Geo. W. Eve, Wm. J. Jefferies.

Mr. L.A. Beardsley is appointed Recorder in place of L.C. Frost, appeared and took his seat.

On motion of Mr. Eve, it was ordered that Mr. Carter be allowed to change the telegraph pole in front of his lot to the opposite side of the Street.

Mr. Morton presented three bills amounting to $21 and upon motion of Mr. Jefferies they were reported to the Overseers of the Poor.

On motion of Mr. Hunter, it was ordered that the Commissioner of the Revenue be authorized to adjust the accounts of Edwin D. Haslup, Wade [H.] Hicks & Mrs. Toombs, with the Collector of taxes.

W.E. Straight offered his resignation as Chamberlain & Clerk of the Council & upon motion of Mr. Eve it was ordered to be laid [up]on the table.

On motion of Mr. Miller it was ordered that the state of the Bridge across the run on Charles Street be reported to the Street Committee and that they be requested to make a report at the next meeting of the Council.[16]

On motion of Mr. Chas. Miller, that the Street Committee be requested to take into their serious consideration the filthy condition of the Streets, and also that they be requested to advertise for bills from persons who will undertake to keep the Streets clean & in order in such a manner as the Committee may direct.

The Council then adjourned.

    [W.E. Straight, Clerk

    Chas. E. Mallam, Mayor]

At a called meeting of the Common Council held at the Council Chamber Thursday Evening July 15th, 1869.

Present– W.E. Nye, Mayor

Geo. W. Eve, L.C. Frost, F. Bauman, W.J. Jefferies, Chas. Miller, Henry Miller, Peter Couse.

P.B. Dunn appointed Common Councilman by Maj. Genl. Canby appeared & was qualified before the Mayor by taking the Oath office & the Oath prescribed by the act of Congress passed July 2nd, 1862, & took his seat at the Board.[17]

W.W. Bowler appointed Councilman by Maj. Genl. Canby having filed his qualification in the Clerk's office appeared and took his seat.

On motion of Mr. Frost, resolved that the Installation of Mr. Barstow as Recorder, now about to be proceeded with, be postponed.

On motion of Mr. Frost, resolved that this body now proceed to recommend one of its own members in accordance with the City Charter to Genl. Canby for appointment as recorder for the City.

On motion of Mr. Frost resolved that Mr. Chas. Miller be recommended to Genl. Canby as Recorder for [of] the City.

On motion of Mr. Frost ordered that the recommendation of Mr. Miller as Recorder be forthwith forwarded to Genl. Canby.

On motion of Mr. Frost ordered that the Chamberlain be directed to pay to Mr. Hart his bill for services as Asst. Comr. of Revenue.

The Mayor presented a communication from Messrs. Braxton & Wallace Attys. in reference to the unpaid interest upon certain Bonds held by Mr. T.S. Coleman and P.[J.] Laurence Stringfellow, and on motion of Mr. Frost it was referred to the Finance Committee to report at the next meeting of the [this] Council.

The Street Committee to whom was referred the unsafe condition of the Bridge across Charles Street asked until the next meeting to make their report, which was granted.

On motion of Mr. Frost, it was authorized that the Chamberlain be authorized to take Council in the matter of the threatened suit of E.H. Taliaferro.

D.S. Dolbar appointed Councilman by Maj. Genl. Canby, appeared and filed his qualifications.

The Council then adjourned.

[W.E. Straight. Clerk

W.E. Nye, Mayor]

The Mayor appointed the following Committees

Finance

W.H. Barstow, D.S. Dolbar

Pub. Property

Geo. W. Eve, W.J. Jefferies, P.B. Dunn

Streets

W.W. Bowler, F. Bauman, L.A. Beardsley, P.B. Dunn

Pumps

Peter Couse, H. Miller

At a regular meeting of the Common Council held at the Council Chamber this Friday evening July 27th 1869.

Present – W.E. Nye, Mayor

W.H. Barstow

D.S. Dolbar, W.J. Jefferies, W.W. Bowler, F. Bauman, Geo. W. Eve, P.B. Dunn.

On motion of Mr. Eve, ordered that the Chamberlain be instructed and authorized to pay the interest for one year, amounting to $120.00 on Bonds held by Mr. S. T. Coleman, also that he be authorized to the interest for three years amounting to $540, due upon Bonds held by P.L. Stringfellow the above amount allowed being collectable under the Stay Law.

The Mayor presented a communication from Robt. A. Taylor in relation to the interest now due on Bonds, referred to the Finance Committee.

On motion of Geo. W. Eve, resolved that the lamp lighter be ordered to turn off the gas in the Street lamp at 12 O'clock.

The Chamberlain presented the petition of Jno. A. Creighton Cartman asking to have refunded to him a portion of the license tax paid by him, and on motion of Mr. Jefferies, it was ordered that the Chamberlain be authorized to receive license tax in proportion to the time the dray may commence upon the Street.

On motion of Mr. Jefferies it was resolved that the services of the present Street Commissioners be dispensed with from this date.

The Mayor presented a communication from Judge Alfred Morton asking if some steps could not be taken to secure some portion of the "Peabody Fund" and on motion of Mr. Eve resolved, that the Mayor, Judge Morton, Maj. Kell[e]y be and are appointed a Committee to present the Claim of this Corporation to a share in the funds recently contributed to the South by Mr. Peabody for Educational purposes.

On motion of Mr. Dolbar, ordered that the Street Committee be authorized to advertise by posting hand bills for bids for persons who will contract to keep the Streets of this Corporation clean for the balance of the present year.

On motion of Mr. Barstow ordered that the matter of repairing the Gunnery Spring be referred to the Pump Committee.

The Chamberlain presented the of Maj. Kelley for advertising amounting to $27.00 and on motion it was ordered to be paid.

The Council then adjourned.

    [W.E. Straight C., Council
    W.E. Nye, Mayor]

At a regular meeting of the Common Council at the Council rooms this Friday evening August 24th 1869.

Present– Wm. E. Nye, Mayor
    W.H. Barstow, Recorder
Councilmen, W.W. Bowler, L.A. Beardsley, F. Bauman, D.S. Dolbar,

Wm. J. Jefferies, P.B. Dunn, Geo. W. Eve.

The Finance Committee to whom was referred the matter of paying the interest upon bonds held by Mr. Richardson for the removal of wrecks from the River, made their report and upon motion of Mr. Eve, their report was ordered to be laid upon the table until the report of a Committee can be heard as to the liability of the Corporation for payment of the[se] Bonds.

On motion of Mr. Couse, it was ordered that the Finance Committee be directed to examine and inquire into the liability of the Corporation for the payment of the above mentioned bonds.

The Street Committee who were directed at the last meeting to advertise for bids from persons who would contract to keep the Streets of the Corporation clean for the balance of the [present] year, Reported that George Aler was the lowest bidder, and that they had partially contracted with him to keep the Streets in order & that Mr. Aler had been at work upon the Streets for several days.

On motion of Mr. Barstow, ordered that the Street Committee be instructed not to make any further payment of money to Mr. Aler for cleaning of the Streets until a contract and bond for the faithful discharge of said work is properly executed and signed.

On motion of Mr. Chas. Miller, the Pump Committee are directed to repair the Gunnery Spring as [may] to them may seem most advisable. On amendment of Mr. Eve, it was ordered that the work done upon said Spring, and all work done for the Corporation, be let to the lowest bidder.

On motion of Mr. Jefferies, it was ordered that the judgment against the Corporation in favor of E.H. Taliaferro for the sum of $16.80 be paid.

A communication from Capt. Quinn & Mr. Reed was presented asking that the Friends of Temperance Society, be allowed the use of the South end room of the Court House in which to hold their meetings, And on motion of Mr. Couse the request was granted, they agreeing to deliver up the same at the pleasure of the Council.[18]

W.E. Straight, Chamberlain, presented a new Bond in the penalty of Ten Thousand dollars, with C.L. Straight & W.E. Nye as his securities [security] and on motion the same was ordered to be accepted, and delivered to the Mayor and by him to be placed in the Bank for safe keeping.

On motion of Mr. Couse, the Street Committee were directed to make enquiries as to the expediency of numbering the Houses of the City.

The Chamberlain presented the bill of Mr. J.W. Adams for stationary furnished the Corporation since April 1868 amounting to $10.10 and on motion it was ordered to be paid.

A bill of 75 cents was presented by Mr. Heinichen for carting dirt from the Street, and on motion it was ordered to be paid.

The Council then adjourned.
[W.E. Straight C., Council
W.E. Nye, Mayor]

At a regular meeting of the Council [held] at the Council Rooms, Tuesday Evening, September 28th, 1869.

Present— W.H. Barstow, Recorder
D.S. Dolbar, W.W. Bowler, Geo. W. Eve, W.J. Jefferies, F. Bauman, Chas. Miller, Peter Couse.

The Finance Committee who were directed at the last meeting to enquire into the liability of the Corporation as to the payment of Bonds given for raising the Wrecks in the river, Reported that they had made a thorough investigation of the matter & in their opinion the Corporation are liable for the payment of the bonds.

On motion of Mr. Eve, ordered that the Chamberlain be directed to pay six months interest to Mr. Richardson upon bonds issued for Wrecks.

The Street Committee to whom was referred the matter of numbering the Streets [houses] of the City, were granted further time to report, and were instructed to ascertain the cost of numbering the houses and report at the next meeting.

The Finance Committee made a written report in regard to the [amount of] interest now due & unpaid by the Corporation & On motion of Mr. Eve, their report was ordered to be recommended to them for further report.

A petition from C.C. Wellford and others asking that foot bridges on Main at the intersection of all the Streets above Commerce, and on motion referred to the Street Committee.[19]

Present— Henry Miller

An amendment of Mr. Eve to Mr. Jefferies' motion, The Night Police salary was fixed at $250.00 per annum.

On motion of Mr. Eve, it was ordered that the Special Police be paid One Dollar per night for their services.

A Bill of Mr. Herndon Council (sic) for the Corporation in the Case of

Taliaferro vs. the Corp. of $5.00 was ordered to be paid.

On motion of Mr. Jefferies [the Motion] fixing the salary of the Night Police was reconsidered.

On motion of Mr. Jefferies, resolved that the Night Police be dispensed with.

On motion of Mr. Eve, ordered that the Chamberlain advertise and receive bids for lighting the Lamps of the City for One Year, Said bids to be submitted to the Council at their next meeting for their approval.

The Council then adjourned.

[W.E. Straight, Clerk
W.H. Barstow, Recorder]

At a regular meeting of the Council held at the Council Rooms Oct. 26th, 1869.

Present– W.E. Nye, Mayor
   W.W. Bowler
   F. Bauman
   H. Miller
   Geo. W. Eve
   P.B. Dunn
   W.J. Jefferies
   W. H. Barstow, Recorder

The Street Committee, who were allowed further time at the last meeting to report in regard to Numbering the Houses of the City, asked for further time in which to report which was granted.

The Finance Committee to whom were allowed further time at the last meeting to make a report of the indebtedness of the Corporation, asked for still further time to make said report, which was granted.

On motion of Mr. Dolber, the Council proceeded to an informal Ballot for Lamp Lighter with the following results:

  John Brown   4 votes
  Hugh Hicks   1 "
  Wash Wright   3 "

After which a formal Ballot was taken By which Washington Wright received 5 and John Brown 3, whereupon Wash. Wright was declared elected, at the salary of $125.00 per annum.

On motion of Mr. Dolbar, it was Ordered that the Lamp lighter light the Street Lamps on all dark nights, when instructed to do so by the Mayor.

A bill presented by Mr. Bowering of $10.00 against the Corporation for making bunks for the Jail was ordered to be paid.

A bill of Capt[ain] Green for $18.50 for blankets furnished for the use of the Jail was ordered to be paid.

A bill presented to Mr. McClain for making ladder for Lamp lighter amounting to $2.50 was ordered to be paid.

P.B. Dunn was appointed a member of the Street Committee in the place of Mr. Beardsley, resigned.

Mr. Wallace asked that the Chamberlain be directed to redeem three One dollar bills issued by the Corporation prior to the War, and on motion the matter was referred to the Finance Committee.

A Petition of the Police to have an increase of salary, and on motion of Mr. Eve it was laid upon the table until the next meeting of the Council.

The Council then adjourned.

[W.E. Straight, Clerk
W.E. Nye, Mayor]

At a Special Meeting of the Council held at the Council Rooms Nov. 15th, 1869.

Present– W.E. Nye, Mayor
W.H. Barstow, Recorder
Chas. Miller, Geo. W. Eve, Wm. J. Jefferies, Peter Couse, P.B. Dunn, W.W. Bowler, D.S. Dolbar.

The Mayor stated to the Council that they had been called together to receive the report of the Finance Committee in regard to the indebtedness of the Corporation and to take some action in regard to appointing Police.

Whereupon Mr. Barstow as Chairman of the Finance Committee presented a written report which upon motion of Mr. Eve, was accepted & ordered to be recorded among the minutes of the [this] meeting.

On motion of Mr. Eve, it was resolved that Mr. Huffman be sent for and asked to attend this meeting, & to report what progress he has made in collecting the taxes of 1868.

On motion of Mr. Barstow, Resolved that the tax Collector be requested to collect as rapidly [as possible] the taxes now due and unpaid and that he destrain against any and all delinquents who shall not have paid their taxes by the 15th Day of December 1869.

The Mayor presented a bill of C.E. Hunter for furnishing Stove pipe for the use of the Jail amounting to $8.05, was ordered to be paid.

On motion of Mr. Eve, Resolved that there be one extra Policeman appointed, to serve as Night Watch and that one of the Day Policemen be designated as Night Watch & that they be paid at the rate of $365.00 per year.

On motion of Mr. Jefferies the resolution fixing the Night Police salary at $365.00 per year was reconsidered.

And a motion of Mr. Miller was put to vote fixing the salary at $500.00 per year, which was lost.

Whereupon the original Motion of Mr. Eve was put, Making the pay of Night Police $365.00 per annum and was carried.

The Council then adjourned.

[W.E. Straight, Clerk

W.H. Barstow, Recorder]

Finance Committee's Report.

Your Finance Committee to whom was referred the matter of ascertaining the present indebtedness of the Corporation would respectfully report– That under an order passed by the Council at a previous meeting, they engaged Mr. Robert Hart to assist the Chamberlain and that together after a most thorough search and examination of the accounts and vouchers in the possession of the present Chamberlain of the Corporation, they have returned to your Committee as the result of their labors the following Statement, which is made up to Jany. 1st 1870.

Total indebtedness of the Corporation $244,521.48 of which (sic)

At a regular meeting of the Council held in [at] the Council Rooms Tuesday Evening November 23rd 1869.

Present– W.E. Nye, Mayor
Peter Couse, W.W. Bowler, Chas. Miller, Henry Miller, P.B. Dunn, W.J. Jefferies.

No q

At a special meeting of the Common Council held at the Council Rooms Monday evening Dec. 13th 1869.

Present– W.E. Nye, Mayor

Geo. W. Eve, Chas. Miller, Wm. J. Jefferies, H. Miller, W.W. Bowler, P.B. Dunn.

Duncan Thompson, Jr. presented an appointment from [Major] Gen[era]l Canby as Chamberlain & Clerk of the Council and it having been certified to this Council that Mr. Thompson has qualified before [Mr.] Eustace Chaffee by taking the several Oaths of Office prescribed by the laws of the State of Virginia together with the oath prescribed by Act of Congress [of] July 2nd, 1862, He is therefore allowed to take his seat as Clerk of this board.

Duncan Thompson appointed Chamberlain by Genl. Canby in place of W. E. Straight who has resigned, presented a bond in the penalty of ten thousand dollars, with Wm. E. Straight, W.E. Nye, H.H. Lamb, Peter Couse & Wm. M. Morrison, and on motion the same was accepted and ordered to be delivered to the Mayor—by him to be placed in the Bank for safe keeping.

Simon Hirsh and Wm. E. Straight appointed Councilmen by [Maj.] Genl. Canby, produced certificates of their due qualification and they were directed to take their seats.

Present– Wm. E. Straight & Simon Hirsh

Mr. Eve presented a bill from B.S. Herndon, M.D. as salary as physician to the Poor House from March 1st 1861 to Dec. 5th 1861, Amt. of Bill $38. On motion of Mr. Eve the bill was ordered to be paid.

A bill from D. Herndon, M.D. was presented for surgical services rendered in the case of Samuel Folk for two weeks attendance, visits and dressing wounds twice per day, Amt. of bill $50.00.

On motion of Mr. Eve, it was ordered that the bill be referred to the Overseers of the Poor.

On motion of Mr. Eve, the Finance Committee were directed to examine the accounts of the late Chamberlain and turn them over to the present Chamberlain.

A communication from Braxton & Wallace was read to the Council requesting the payment of three year's interest, amounting to Eighteen hundred Dollars, on the Bonds of the Corporation, owned by Thomas Hill, Administrator of George Ficklen. On motion of W.E. Straight, the matter was laid over until next meeting.

On motion of Mr. Eve the resolution passed at the last meeting of the Council directing the Collector of taxes to destrain for all taxes not paid by the 15th of December, was amended so as to read the 15th of January.

The Council then adjourned.

[Duncan Thompson, Clerk

W.E. Nye, Mayor]

At a regular meeting of the Common Council held at the Council Rooms Tuesday evening Decr. 28th, 1869.

Present– W.E. Nye, Mayor
Peter Couse, Geo. W. Eve, Wm. J. Jefferies, Wm. E. Straight, Simon Hirsh, F. Bauman, Henry Miller, Chas. Miller.

The Finance Committee appointed to examine the accounts of the late Chamberlain made the following report, That, in accordance with the direction of the Council they have examined the accounts and books of the late Chamberlain W.E. Straight and find the same correct in all respects and a balance of $960.60 [$915.60] in his hands of Corporation money, which amount with the books he has turned over to Duncan Thompson, Jr. the present Chamberlain.

On motion of Mr. Eve, the report was accepted.

A communication from Braxton & Wallace (requesting the payment of interest on bonds held by Thomas Hill, Administrator of Geo. Ficklen, Decd.), which was laid over at the last meeting, was taken up and after some discussion it was ordered on motion of Mr. Straight that the communication be referred to the Finance Committee and on motion of Mr. Eve the Mayor was requested to act with the Committee.

Mr. St. Geo. Fitzhugh appeared before the Council and requested the sale of property belonging to the Corporation situated on Main Street.

On motion of Mr. W.E. Straight the matter of the sale of said property was referred to the Property Committee to report at the next meeting.

The following appointments were made by the Mayor—Simon Hirsh on St[reet] Committee; W.E. Straight on Finance Committee; Chas. Miller on Pub[lic] Property Committee.

On motion of W.E. Straight, it was ordered that the Street Committee be directed to have the Street on [the corner of] Winchester & Amelia Strts. repaired at once.

On motion of Mr. Eve, it was ordered that the Street Committee be directed to examine the damage done on Charles Street by waste water from Mr. Marye's Mill race and request Mr. Marye to repair the damage immediately.

On motion of Mr. Jefferies it was resolved by the Common Council that the name of William Street be changed to Caroline [Commerce] and the name of Caroline Street be changed to Main St.

On motion of Charles Miller the Street Committee was then directed to enquire into and ascertain the probable cost of putting up the names of the Streets at the corners and numbering [of] the houses and report at the next meeting, showing samples of the lettering numbering [numbers] &c.

On motion of Mr. Eve the Mayor was requested to procure a Street lamp to replace one that is broken.

Johnston & Co. presented a Bill to the Council for Coal, Oil &c Amounting to $13.72.

On motion of Mr. Jefferies it was ordered to be paid.

James McGuire presented a bill for sundry articles purchased by the Corporation amounting to Four dollars & Twenty cents. On motion of Mr. Eve it was ordered to be paid.

Markey presented a bill for blankets amounting to Thirty two dollars. On motion of Mr. Eve it was laid over until the next meeting.

The Council then adjourned.

    [Duncan Thompson

    W.E. Nye

    C.C. Mayor]

∽ NOTES ∾

1. The Market Square was located behind the Town Hall/Market House in the 900 block of Princess Anne Street and was where Confederate General William Barksdale had made his headquarters during the street fighting on December 11, 1862, during the opening phase of the battle of Fredericksburg. Mercer Square was an area just west of the town proper where the Federal attacks occurred two days later, on December 13th.

2. The municipal gas works was located on the Rappahannock River, downstream from the commercial wharves.
3. Commerce and Main Streets, in 1862, were originally named William and Caroline Streets and these names have been returned to use. This particular intersection is the heart of the central business district. William Street extends east, to a bridge over the Rappahannock River, and west, into Spotsylvania County and beyond. Caroline Street in that area primarily commercial in nature, with some residential units above storefronts.
4. The Peabody Education Fund had been set up in 1867-68 by a Massachusetts financier named George Peabody, who was interested in educational philanthropy. The fund was set up for the "education of destitute children of the Southern States," but was to be used to strengthen existing schools rather than to set up new ones. As a consequence, newly freed slaves would not benefit from Mr. Peabody's generosity. Barnas Sears was the agent for administering the fund and established his office in Staunton.
5. There is no accompanying map in the Council records.
6. A sink in this context is a privy, or a cesspool.
7. Greenback was a term given to paper money printed with green ink and issued by the United States government to help fund the Civil War. The Legal Tender Act, passed in February 1862, authorized $150 million to be printed without being backed by gold or silver. Instead, its value was maintained by confidence and faith in the government that issued it. Another $300 million was issued in 1863.
8. Dr. Wellford's house was in the 700 block of Princess Anne Street.
9. Major General John M. Schofield, West Point class of 1853, was the military governor of the First Military District, which encompassed the state of Virginia. He had fought in the Western Theater and helped to destroy the Confederate Army of Tennessee as Sherman marched to the sea. A few months after this correspondence, he would appointed Secretary of War, when President Andrew Johnson forced the wartime Secretary, Edwin Stanton, out of that position.
10. Lieutenant Hector Sears was a Union volunteer who had been wounded in battle in 1863 and later been commissioned in the Veteran Reserve Corps, to serve in the Freedmen's Bureau. Within the First Military District, Lt. Sears served in the Sixth Subdistrict, which included

Fredericksburg as well as Spotsylvania, Stafford, and King George Counties. The oath being referred to came out of Congressional legislation passed on July 2, 1862. Radical Republicans developed an oath of allegiance for federal employees, which they also used after the war to remove former Confederates from politics. The required oath, which both President Lincoln and Johnson had opposed, stated that the oath taker had never voluntarily borne arms against the United States and had not voluntarily given aid to, or even encouraged those who had engaged in hostilities.

11. Peter Couse was the son of a New Jersey family that had moved to Spotsylvania County in 1840. They settled at a place called Laurel Hill, near Spotsylvania Court House, and were part of a small enclave of people who remained loyal to the Union when the war came. Another enclave of Unionists were located in the Salem Church area and some of them actually spied for Union forces. Peter was arrested by Confederate authorities in March 1862 and imprisoned in Richmond. Upon his release, in September, he returned North for the duration. After the war, he and his family settled in Fredericksburg and his appointment to the Common Council was a small part of Radical Reconstruction, wherein military authorities attempted to remove rebellious elements from politics. A fascinating diary written by Katherine Couse was published in the 2002 volume of *Fredericksburg History and Biography,* in an article called "Between the Lines: The Diary of a Unionist Woman at the Battle of Spotsylvania Court House."

12. Colonel Charles E. Mallam had been a Union soldier and represented the federal government's desire to create a more representative government in the South. Local newspapers routinely reported on local politics and provide more comments than are contained in the of official Council minutes. The *Fredericksburg Ledger* for May 1, 1868 reported that Colonel Mallam took the oath of citizenship of Virginia, an anti-dueling oath, the oath of office for mayor, and the iron-clad oath of 1862 testifying he had not borne arms against the United States government.

13. The fair grounds were the area just west of the town proper, where Federal attacks had been made against Marye's Heights. The site was also referred to as Mercer Square. At one point in 1866, Federal authorities had considered establishing the Fredericksburg National Cemetery there, where there were already mass burials of Union soldiers killed in December 1862. The

new cemetery was established atop the heights instead. When the mass graves were disinterred, workers did not fill in the open pits and the area remains something of a mess for years. See Noel G. Harrison, *Fredericksburg Civil War Sites* (Lynchburg, 1995), pp. 30-33.

14. The tax structure reflects an emphasis on minimizing taxes on wealth and placing as much of the burden on persons engaged in trades, etc. The personal property tax, for instance, puts a burden on those who use tools to make a living. Similarly, a tax of three dollars on males over the age of 21, put a real burden on former slaves. These strategies were not unique to Fredericksburg, but practiced throughout the defeated South.

15. Railroad construction in the South was given considerable attention after the Civil War. Francis H. Pierpont, the Provisional Governor of Virginia, had strongly supported reconstruction of Virginia railways and this effort continued with his successor, Henry H. Wells. Major General Schofield had appointed Wells as Provisional Governor on April 4, 1868.

16. This bridge would have been located in the 200 block of Charles Street, south of the railway tracks.

17. Major General Edward Richard Sprigg Canby had taken charge of the First Military District in April 1869. He was a career soldier, West Point class of 1839, and had seen Civil War service. He was considered an excellent administrator.

18. Captain Silvanus J. Quinn had come to Fredericksburg during the Civil War with the 13th Mississippi Regiment. He returned to marry a local girl and is buried in the Fredericksburg Cemetery. He served in a variety of civic capacities and also wrote *The History of the City of Fredericksburg, Virginia*, published in 1908. National Park historian Mac Wyckoff wrote a brief article on Quinn called "Silvanus Jackson Quinn: Warrior, Public Servant, and Fredericksburg Historian," published in the 2006 volume of *Fredericksburg History and Biography*.

19. The area "above" Commerce (now William) Street was the north end of town and the site of numerous mills. Bridges were needed across the various tail races, the outflow of the water streams that powered the different industries.

Post war photograph of Charles Miller's store, at the corner of William and Liberty Streets. View is looking across Liberty Street to William Street. Photo from the collection of Mrs. Jerry H. Brent.

Modern view of what is today 600 William Street. View is looking across William Street to Liberty Street. The door and two windows in the wall to the left are visible in the historic photo above.

A Murder in Fredericksburg

By Elizabeth Parnicza

By all accounts, the darkness that fell in Fredericksburg on May 25, 1865 was remarkable. In the streets of Liberty Town, just west of downtown Fredericksburg, one man said he could only see six steps in front of him. The dark night would obscure the events and identities associated with a fatal occurrence.

As the church bells tolled nine, 25-year-old August Ebert sat in the darkness beside a "colored boy" on the pavement outside Charles Miller's store at the corner of Commerce Street and Liberty Street (modern address 600 William Street). He watched four Union soldiers enter his sometime employer's shop. First, one man pushed open the door and walked inside. Three more arrived soon afterward.[1]

Inside the shop, a typical Thursday night scene played out. Charles Miller's older brother George had walked in earlier, remarking that if the weather was good, he would plant Charles' lot the next morning. Louis Kruger, a Baltimore resident who helped Charles mind the shop, walked into the store proper from an adjoining room just after the soldiers entered. Charles Miller attended the soldiers, who had quietly gathered in the store. The first man asked for a quart of cherries and the four soldiers sat at the counter and ate them. Another soldier called for a round of cigars, which the shopkeeper distributed. When they finished the cherries, a soldier asked for an orange apiece, and Mr. Kruger obliged.

The first soldier stated the price for the fare: 50 cents. Charles Miller objected; the price for all the goods was 70 cents. The soldier disagreed. He was only prepared to pay for the cherries and oranges, which came to a total of 50 cents, leaving the cigars as his friend's responsibility. When the shopkeeper agreed, it seemed the matter was settled as the soldier reached to pay for the goods.

Post war photo of Charles Miller's store. View is looking across Liberty Street. Photo from the collection of Mrs. Jerry H. Brent.

Drawing his hand back from his pocket, the soldier changed his mind, declaring: "Oh well, charge it to Uncle Sam!"

"Uncle Sam had nothing to do with that. That thing was played out, whoever calls for an article must pay for it himself!" the shopkeeper rejoined. Two of the soldiers had made an exit during the conversation. The two others started for the door. George Miller asked his brother in German if they should hold the men until they paid for the articles, but Charles responded in German: "Never mind. Let them alone. I do not want to interfere with them." The shopkeeper later said that he did not want any trouble.

Charles Miller went for his coat and walked out saying in German, "I will see about it, whether Uncle Sam pays for them articles or not." George said that he would go along on his way home as his brother Charles sought a guard. Mr. Kruger stood in the shop's doorway as he, Mr. Ebert, and the young unknown boy watched the brothers disappear into the darkness.[2]

A relative calm ensued for several minutes until August Ebert heard a cry in the night. He described it as a groaning, "hallo," and with the young boy and Mr. Kruger, he struck out down Commerce Street to determine its source. About 25 steps down the street, they found George Miller supporting himself with his hands on the brick Masonic Cemetery wall, crying out in the darkness. When he saw a friendly face, he called out: "Mr. Kruger, oh help me in the house!"[3]

The two men brought George Miller into the residential portion of the store and laid him on the floor, face down, with a bag under his head. The men washed the blood from the back of his head and cut the hair away from the wound. He had a serious gash on the back of his head and was in so much pain that he believed himself shot. The injured man declared that he was willing to die because he thought that he was hurt too badly to live and keep his senses.[4]

Charles Miller returned with a guard to find his brother suffering from the grievous injury. As he went back out into the streets, a lieutenant approached and asked if he wanted a doctor. Charles pled for him to find a doctor to see to his brother. A short time later, Dr. Edward F. Dodge, assistant surgeon to the 19th Wisconsin Volunteers, arrived to examine George and dressed and sutured his wound. The doctor left when he finished, intending to check in again the next morning.

Between one and two o'clock in the morning, as Charles Miller sat up with his brother, George became unresponsive. Charles touched his brother's hands and noticed they were cold. His feet and face were cold as well. Though his body was still warm, they sent for the doctor, who confirmed their fears. George had died.[5]

In the next morning's light, Louis Kruger found George's cap on Commerce Street, a silent witness to the evening's tragedy. There were no living witnesses but the guilty. The testimony that would bring to light the events of May 25 found its source in a most unlikely individual, a man of humble means and little status who was not even present at the attack.

This incident was not the first time that the Civil War had intruded into Charles Miller's life. He and his brother were German immigrants, who had been living in Fredericksburg less than five years. Charles owned several vacant lots adjacent to his store and on the edge of town. In May 1864, some of his land had become the temporary resting place for the bodies of 328 Union soldiers, casualties from the fighting at Spotsylvania Court House. A year later almost to the day, Union soldiers had killed George Miller, who had intended to plant one of the lots around the buried soldiers the next day.[6]

Charles and George Miller's 1865 entanglement with the United States Army was connected to the Union Sixth Corps, which was passing through Fredericksburg on its way to Washington D.C. for discharge. Although the rest of the Army of the Potomac and elements of the Army of Georgia and the Army of the Tennessee had already passed through Fredericksburg on their way to the Grand Review in the capital, the Sixth Corps had remained behind near Danville, chasing bands of marauders, disarming remaining pockets of Confederate soldiers, and escorting Confederate government property northward. The Sixth Corps missed the Grand Review on May 23. They were transferred from Danville to Richmond by rail, and the bulk of its troops marched through Fredericksburg on May 29.[7]

Considering the Sixth Corps' timeline, the attack on George and Charles Miller preceded the arrival of the main body of the corps by four days. The troops involved must have either been part of an advance guard or had ventured ahead without permission. The investigation to find the responsible parties began immediately the next morning, and the Provost Guard sought to identify the four soldiers who had entered Charles Miller's store the night before.

Events moved quickly after the brothers left the shop. On May 31, 1865, Charles Miller's testimony before the court martial provided as much detail as the darkness allowed on the ambush that followed:

The one who called for the cherries and one of the last three which came in and walked out there & crossed the street myself and my brother walked out and went down [the] street on the same side where I lived. While we were walking down the street the two which I saw cross the street recrossed the street. I heard nothing of them except that when we were near the middle of the graveyard on the street they came close to us, about 5 or 6 feet of us nearly as I can guess and one of them said 'Tap' so much as I could understand. At the same time as soon as they said that word there was two bricks thrown at myself and my brother, my brother was knocked down at once, and one brick struck me very slight on my elbow. I then jumped to the left hand side out into the road trying to escape. Two more bricks were thrown after me but did not strike me. I hallowed once 'Guard' to try to stop them from following me up.[8]

Escaping the pursuing soldiers, Charles Miller made it to the Provost Guard's headquarters, but they failed to locate the men responsible for the attack that evening. Charles returned to the shop to find his brother grievously wounded in the head and retrieved by Louis Kruger, August Ebert, and the young boy who had been sitting outside the shop. After his brother passed away, it became imperative to find the soldiers who had, intentionally or unintentionally, killed an innocent citizen.

Lieutenant Alonzo H. Russell, of the 19th Wisconsin Infantry, had charge of the Provost Guard in Fredericksburg. Based on descriptions provided by Charles Miller and Louis Kruger, he arrested four men: James Lynch, of Company A, 61st Pennsylvania Infantry; Amos Fielding, Company C, 61st Pennsylvania Infantry; John Wilson, Company G, 67th Pennsylvania Infantry; and William Irvin, Company D, 67th Pennsylvania Infantry. All of them were from the Army of the Potomac's Sixth Corps.

The Provost Guard questioned Louis Kruger to verify the identities of the men in his custody. Mr. Kruger remembered Amos Fielding wearing a white handkerchief, and he recollected William Irvin by his teeth, which must have been distinctive. Earlier in the day, Irvin had treated Fielding to a fresh, white handkerchief, and John Wilson wore a clean one to match. Further witness identification was rendered unnecessary when the first accused, James Lynch, identified all four of them as having been in Miller's store on the night of the incident.[9]

James Lynch was a Philadelphia native who had been wounded in the right hand at the Wilderness, in May 1864. During his recovery, he had left the hospital to visit home, where he was arrested for desertion. Lynch could not sign his own name, but made his mark on all of his documentation.[10]

Amos Fielding was 23 years old, with dark hair, gray eyes, and a light complexion. He had enlisted in Pittsburgh and been wounded in May 1862 at Fair Oaks. He had deserted the army on May 4, 1864 during the army's march to the Rapidan River, at the beginning of what would be called the Overland Campaign. Fielding was caught in Pittsburgh and returned to his regiment. At some point, he hired an African American camp servant and cook named Doctor Galland.[11]

A 22-year-old with gray eyes and black hair, John Wilson had been born in Ireland and worked as a laborer in America. He had agreed to serve as a substitute for Thomas Farney, who had been drafted in December 1864. He proved a poor soldier and spent January and February 1865 absent without leave. When he returned in March, he was sentenced to forfeit $10 of his pay for two months. In six months of service, this incident in Fredericksburg was already Private Wilson's second court martial.[12]

The final soldier on trial was William Irvin, a 21-year-old former laborer who stood 5 feet 9 inches tall, and had hazel hair and gray eyes. He had enlisted as a substitute in Carlisle, Pennsylvania in December 1864 and deserted the army on April 30, 1865 near Washington D.C. He had been caught and placed in confinement.[13]

One side of the brick cemetery wall remains intact. The brick building to the right was constructed after the graves were relocated to another nearby Masonic burying ground.

Of the accused, James Lynch was the only soldier not previously convicted of desertion or being absent without leave. He took the stand first and delivered a detailed and clear testimony that cleared him of wrongdoing and pinned accusations elsewhere. According to Private Lynch, William Irvin and John Wilson were the first to enter the store, and Wilson intended to treat them all. Wilson had called for all of the articles.

James Lynch was the first one to leave the store, with Amos Fielding right behind him. Private Lynch claimed they crossed two streets and stood on a corner. Soon, they saw Privates Irvin and Wilson, and "one Citizen" coming out of the store, crossing the street and continuing toward the river. John Wilson came back to pick up a brick, chased after the citizen, and struck the man down. James Lynch said he heard John Wilson say something to the effect that, "he stopped that man from following him."[14] When Private Wilson followed in taking the witness stand, he claimed that he could not remember many of the details of that night. There was no disturbance, nor did he hear any dispute about payment for the articles ordered and consumed. Throughout the trial, several witnesses were asked if they noticed that members of the party had exchanged hats or caps. While James Lynch claimed that he thought William Irvin wore Amos Fielding's hat the next morning, John Wilson said he had not changed hats, and nor had anyone else.[15]

While the picture James Lynch painted was clearer and placed blame largely on the shoulders of one of the party, it was not the full story. John Wilson's vague testimony did little to refute the charges that now appeared strongly against him. The verdict hinged on testimony from a man more likely to have been overlooked. The camp servant Doctor Galland rose to testify—"Doctor" was his first name, not a title. He must have presented both an unusual figure on the stand and been a deep surprise to the soldiers on trial. Mr. Galland was an African American in the employ of accused soldier Amos Fielding. He would be able to relate the words and actions of the accused in the immediate aftermath of the incident.

Like countless camp servants in the Army of the Potomac, Mr. Galland's background and future remain a mystery. He held little to no status, perhaps a former slave escaping to freedom or a free man looking for work. As he was sworn in by the court on June 2, 1865, however, Mr. Galland's story had the power to clear a man's name and reveal the threads of guilt among the accused soldiers. Through his testimony, we perceive a man who was perhaps not well-educated, but courageous enough to speak with clarity and determination.

On the evening of May 25, lying on a pallet in the upstairs room that members of the 61st Pennsylvania were occupying in downtown Fredericksburg, Doctor Galland saw his employer, Amos Fielding, return with another soldier. Next to Galland in the room that night was a friend named Mr. Stevens, whose identity is unknown, but could have been a fellow camp servant. Mr. Galland testified to the actions of Amos Fielding's companion as they entered the room: "He jerked my Kiver off me & kicked me. Then Mr Fielding told him not to do that I was his cook. He said G_ D_ the Nigger, he aint no more than no other d-n nigger. Mr Fielding told him by God dont he do that no how and he said he dont care about no d-d nigger."[16]

There is no known record of how long Doctor Galland had served Amos Fielding, but Fielding clearly showed some loyalty in defending his cook, though it seems a half-hearted attempt. The soldier who accompanied Fielding showed nothing but contempt, swearing at and kicking him in order to procure better sleeping arrangements. After this vicious treatment of a camp servant, Amos Fielding and the assailant settled in to sleep. They were talking to one another when Doctor Galland fell asleep. The next morning, Mr. Galland woke to hear them continuing their conversation: "Mr Fielding he asked the man what he was going to say says he by God I aint going to know nothing about it. Then Fielding said you aint going to know nothing about it. He said no. Mr. Fielding said By God we gave him his dose, we fixed him."[17]

In the context of the previous evening's events, these words were far from innocent musings. Shortly after he overheard this conversation, as Doctor Galland would testify, Lieutenant Russell of the Provost Guard climbed the stairs to the room, and Fielding and his fellow soldier ducked into a side room. Lieutenant Russell announced that he knew who was responsible for the events of the night before and that he wanted everyone to get up and put on their hats.

The lieutenant's command to put on hats must have made the soldiers realize that their clothing could give them away if the civilians in Miller's shop remembered any of the distinctive features about the soldiers in the store. Once Lieutenant Russell went back downstairs, the two soldiers came out of the side room. Amos Fielding changed hats with a sergeant. Fielding's comrade took Doctor Galland's hat and left his, a black "hat with cross seams." Mr. Stevens, Galland's friend who had slept beside him that night, warned him that Fielding and the other soldier were accused of breaking into a shop. He said that Galland may not want to wear the newly exchanged hat. Doctor Galland took the advice, and when he appeared in front of the lieutenant bare-headed, he stated that Fielding's companion had taken his hat.

Lieutenant Russell could draw reasonable conclusions from Doctor Galland's story, and it must have proved galling to the soldiers to be given away by an individual they considered quite beneath their status. Intimidation against Doctor Galland continued to the very day of the trial, when William Irvin, standing trial alongside Amos Fielding, said to Mr. Galland as he walked past, "God damn you I'll murder you." Despite this threat and his presence in Miller's shop that evening, Private Irvin was not the companion who came back with Amos Fielding the night of the murder and kicked Doctor Galland.[18]

The mystery soldier's identity was not revealed until a second court martial convened the day after the first one had concluded. As James Lynch and John Wilson went on trial, Doctor Galland identified Lynch as the soldier who had kicked him off his pallet and taken his cap. Private Lynch

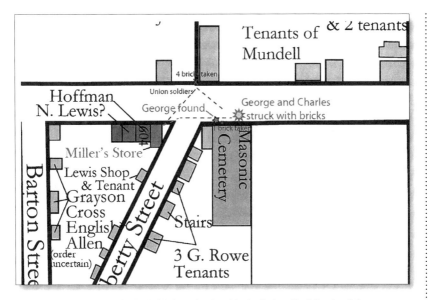

Detail from a map of Civil War Fredericksburg developed by the National Park Service. Crime scene details added by the author.

had spent his time on the witness stand in the earlier trial trying to establish John Wilson as the guilty party. Amos Fielding had corroborated his testimony, and James Lynch reiterated his account at the second court martial. At both hearings, however, Doctor Galland had coolly dismantled the testimony of these white soldiers, upsetting the established hierarchy and shifting the scales of guilt in their direction.[19]

How must Doctor Galland have felt in taking the stand against his employer and other United States soldiers, setting his own future on an uncertain path? The trial clearly hinged on the validity of his testimony and had put the case against at least three of the soldiers back on firm footing. Adding fuel to Mr. Galland's fire, further questioning of Charles Miller led to more details about the bricks used in the attack. Mr. Miller claimed that four bricks were thrown, without time enough between throwing the first pair of bricks and the second pair for the men to stop to pick up more bricks. The attack could not have been the act of one man.

Multiple witnesses noted a stack of loose bricks on Alexander's Corner, diagonally across from Miller's shop, as well as a brick missing from the cemetery wall. These locations were clearly the sources of the bricks used as weapons in the attack. The next morning, four bricks were found near

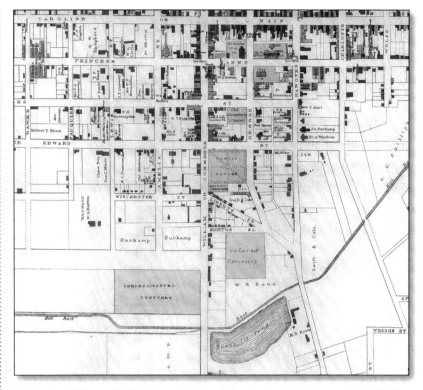

Portion of an 1878 map of Fredericksburg. The Masonic Cemetery just below the area labeled "Public Square" is where straggling Union soldiers attacked George Miller. Charles Miller's store is just below the cemetery, at the apex of the lot at William and Liberty Streets. The map is turned 90 degrees from the map on page 111.

where George Miller had fallen. James Lynch's story of John Wilson acting as the lone brick-thrower simply could not hold up to Charles Miller's account that specified the number of bricks and the speed at which they were thrown.[20]

The court martial that had convened on June 1, 1865 included the charge that William Irvin and Amos Fielding did, "maliciously and unlawfully take the life of George Miller a Citizen of the City of Fredericksburg, Va." Both soldiers pled not guilty and the court heard testimony for two days. The next trial brought the charge that James Lynch did, "unlawfully and maliciously aid and abet in taking the life of George Miller." John Wilson was brought to both trials, but charges were not specified against him at either one.

A standout among the witnesses, Doctor Galland offered pivotal testimony. His words refuted James Lynch's testimony against John Wilson and identified Lynch as a suspicious individual along with the other men. The resulting verdict demonstrated that the courts gave validity to Mr. Galland's testimony over Private Lynch's— trusting the black man's word over a white man's.

William Irvin, Amos Fielding, and James Lynch were all found guilty of manslaughter, recognizing that George Miller's death had not been premeditated. John Wilson alone escaped a court ruling. All three soldiers were sentenced to three years of hard labor and "confined to solitary confinement on Bread & water during the first ten days of each month of the first year." All three of the guilty soldiers also suffered "loss of all pay or allowances due or to become due him from the United States." For reasons unknown, Amos Fielding's sentence was remitted in November 1865, and he was sent back to Harrisburg, Pennsylvania to be mustered out of the army.[21]

In the aftermath of George Miller's death, word spread through the Union army, causing at least one soldier to remark on a slight stir in the army's ranks. Private Stephen W. Gordon, of the 15th New Jersey Infantry, wrote in his diary on May 29, 1865: "There was about two thousand of our Corps straggled ahead and got in the town. Some of them murdered a Merchant of the town. They was all arrested and sent to Washington." Although he was not correct in the details of the case, Gordon's words indicate a desired separation between the disciplined soldiers in the ranks and the untrustworthy soldiers who had "straggled ahead" and committed crimes.[22]

The *Fredericksburg Ledger* alerted the Fredericksburg community of the news and lamented George Miller's death, stating: "Mr. Miller has been residing here for several years, and was regarded as a peaceable and quiet citizen." Beyond his legacy as a "peaceable and quiet citizen," George Miller left behind a wife and several children. His death was recollected in public memory as recently as 1987, in a *Fredericksburg Times* article. The recounted story claimed that he was struck by Union soldiers throwing bricks in December 1862. Though the family's memory mistakenly associated George Miller's death with the Battle of Fredericksburg, it is worth noting that 122 years after the fact, they correctly connected his fate to bricks in the hands of Union soldiers.[23]

In the years following the incident, the 1870 Census shows 38-year-old Charles Miller, his wife Catherine, and their six children still residing in Fredericksburg. Charles Miller's shop continued its use as a grocery store through the turn of the century. Charles Miller had listed his place of birth as Hanover, Prussia. The census records also show another family of Millers living in Fredericksburg, headed by 44-year-old Sophia, with four children, all born in Hanover, Germany. Connected by last name, proximity of age, and birthplace, it is likely that this was George Miller's family. One son was named George, then 15 and working in a woolen mill. By 1880, widowed Sophia and son George had moved to Baltimore and were living with daughter Henrietta and her family. Sophia later became a boarder in Baltimore and died in 1903. She never remarried.[24]

In the tragic events of May 25, 1865, we see the dark underside of war. Enjoying fruit and cigars, the four soldiers crossed the line to abuse civilians. Perhaps the men had fallen prey to common prejudices of the times against immigrants or individuals with German backgrounds. Perhaps seeing the Miller brothers strike out for a provost guard threatened their approaching release from the army, and they panicked. Whatever caused the men's reactions, the future of both Miller families was shattered in a few fateful moments. Stephen Gordon asserted that the soldiers who had committed the murder were stragglers. Their nonchalant attitude and dismissal of a shopkeeper's right to be paid for his goods certainly indicate the mentality of those operating outside the bounds of army discipline.[25]

A civilian's murder at the hands of the Union army was not a promising entrance to postwar life in Fredericksburg and foreshadowed the nation's struggle with reunion. Those years witnessed not only George Miller's death at the hands of Federal soldiers, but also the death of an occupying soldier attacking a civilian in July 1865 and the death of a couple supposedly robbed and killed by members of the Burial Corps in 1866. Peace in the Fredericksburg area had a rocky beginning, with high tensions between groups negotiating authority in the post-war South.[26]

Of all those who participated in the trial, Doctor Galland's role reveals aspects of a different society to come. The court's validation of Mr. Galland's statements promised a future that recognized the humanity and integrity of a black man. His courage in taking the stand to represent the truth demonstrated a measure of hope in the dark trial, but the road to equality for African Americans would be long and difficult. If Mr. Galland was indeed a former slave, this may have been his first opportunity to stand up against injustice. That he did so despite death threats shows a deep moral character.

The period of growth in African American institutions and rights would be short-lived during Reconstruction, but individuals like Doctor Galland represented the promise of the future. The prevailing darkness on May 25, 1865, however, would hang over Fredericksburg for years to come.[27]

∽ NOTES ∾

1. Court Martial for William Irvin, John Wilson, and Amos Fielding, May 28, 1865, NARA File #mm-3131, August Ebert testimony, 37-46; Charles Miller's shop still stands today at 600 William Street.
2. Court Martial for William Irvin, John Wilson, and Amos Fielding, May 28, 1865, NARA File #mm-3131, Charles Miller's testimony, 5-20.
3. This wall belonged to the second Masonic Cemetery in Fredericksburg. In 1799, Fredericksburg's Masonic Lodge split over political differences, leading the new lodge–American Lodge #63–to purchase its own plot for a burying ground in 1804, at the corner of Liberty St. and William St., adjacent to the City Cemetery and across the street from Miller's store. In 1954, when Sears & Roebuck purchased the land to construct a store, the remains were re-interred at the first Masonic Cemetery.
4. Court Martial for William Irvin, John Wilson, and Amos Fielding, May 28, 1865, NARA File #mm-3131, testimony of Louis Kruger, Dr. E. F. Dodge, and August Ebert, 20-44
5. Ibid., Charles Miller's testimony, 5-20.
6. "A Quarter-Century of Research on Fredericksburg's 'Burial of the Dead' Photographs, Part 2," Mysteries and Conundrums, Noel Harrison, accessed July 30, 2016, https://npsfrsp.wordpress.com/2016/03/27/a-quarter-century-of-research-on-fredericksburgs-burial-of-the-dead-photographs-part-2/; U.S. Quartermaster General's Office, Statement of the Disposition of Some of the Bodies of Deceased Union Soldiers and Prisoners of War Whose Remains have been Removed to National Cemeteries…4 Washington, 1869): 26; Noel G. Harrison, Victims and Survivors: New Perspectives on Fredericksburg's May 1864 Photographs, Military Images, Nov.-Dec. 1998: 12, 15.

7. Noel Harrison authored an excellent blog post detailing the movements of various army units passing through Fredericksburg prior to the Grand Review: "William T. Sherman at Spotsylvania, Chancellorsville, and Fredericksburg, May 1865," Noel Harrison, accessed August 13, 2016, https://npsfrsp.wordpress.com/2015/05/04/william-t-sherman-at-spotsylvania-chancellorsville-and-fredericksburg-may-1865/; *The War of the Rebellion: A Compilation of Official Records of the Union and Confederate Armies, (Washington, D.C., 1890-1901), Series I., Vol. 46, Part 3, 1081-1082, 1120, 1128-1129, 1135-1136, 1155-1156, 1197, 1199-1200, 1212.*
8. Court Martial for William Irvin, John Wilson, and Amos Fielding, May 28, 1865, NARA File #mm-3131, Charles Miller's testimony, 7-8.
9. Ibid., Louis Kruger's testimony, 30-31; Ibid., James Lynch's testimony, 46-47.
10. James Lynch, Co. A 61st Pennsylvania Infantry, Compiled Military Service Record, NARA.
11. Amos Fielding, Co. C 61st Pennsylvania Infantry, Compiled Military Service Record, NARA.
12. James Wilson, Co. G 67th Pennsylvania Infantry, Compiled Military Service Record, NARA.
13. William Irvin (Irvine), Co. D 67th Pennsylvania Infantry, Compiled Military Service Record, NARA.
14. Court Martial for William Irvin, John Wilson, and Amos Fielding, May 28, 1865, NARA File #mm-3131, James Lynch's testimony, 46-54.
15. Ibid., James Wilson's testimony, 55-60.
16. Ibid., Doctor Galland's testimony, 60-68.
17. Ibid., Doctor Galland's testimony, 60-68.
18. Ibid., Doctor Galland's testimony, 60-68.
19. Court Martial for James Lynch and John Wilson, NARA File: oo-926, 10-11.
20. Court Martial for William Irvin, John Wilson, and Amos Fielding, May 28, 1865, NARA File #mm-3131; Some discrepancy remains in the number of bricks thrown and found. While Miller's testimony was clear that four bricks were thrown and four were found, he lists four red bricks being found taken from Alexander's corner and one brick from the cemetery wall, totaling five.

21. Court Martial for William Irvin, John Wilson, and Amos Fielding, May 28, 1865, NARA File #mm-3131, 73; Court Martial for James Lynch and John Wilson, NARA File: oo-926, 18; "Findings of the Military Commission," *New Era (Fredericksburg, Va.), July 14, 1865;* Court Martial for William Irvin, John Wilson, and Amos Fielding, May 28, 1865, NARA File #mm-3131, 74.
22. Gordon, Stephen W., diary entry for May 29, 1865, in FRSP collection.
23. "Murder Committed—A Citizen Killed—Detectives on the Track of the Murderers," *Fredericksburg Ledger, May 26, 1865;* "'Times' Building Reflects Heritage of Liberty Town," Fredericksburg Times, September 1987.
24. U.S. Census.
25. For a comprehensive study of United States Army policy toward violence and hard war during the Civil War, see Mark Grimsley, *Hard Hand of War.*
26. "A Federal Soldier Killed," *Fredericksburg Ledger, July 20, 1865;* "A Most Diabolical Murder. Man and Wife Killed near Fredericksburg. The Woman's Body Burnt in Her own House! [From the Fredericksburg Herald of yesterday.]," Richmond Whig, August 31, 1866.
27. For a thorough consideration of race relations in postwar America, see David Blight, *Race and Reunion.*

Photo of Sunken Road from the 12th Rhode Island Infantry's regimental history. The house in the middle background is not a wartime structure.

Modern view showing the intact stone wall and the Innis House, also visible in the historic photo above.

Southern Exposure

By Noel G. Harrison and Erik Nelson

The 12th Rhode Island Volunteer Infantry was a nine-month regiment. They were recruited during the manpower crisis that occurred in the summer of 1862 and saw combat at Fredericksburg in December. Short-term units like the 12th Rhode Island illustrate the conflict between the federal government's need for a reliable fighting force and the militia traditions that harkened back to the nation's colonial past. These tensions would eventually result in a national military draft, but in 1862, the federal government still had to rely on volunteers coming forward to defend the republic and some of them were not willing to commit to a longer enlistment.

After Fort Sumter, President Abraham Lincoln had called for 75,000 men for three months' service. The rebellion of the Southern states proved to be something more than short-term troops could handle and a call soon went out for volunteers to serve for three years. Major General George B. McClellan organized and trained the incoming surge of men into a huge Federal force that he named the Army of the Potomac, but he lacked the nerve to engage in active operations during 1861. He planned to fight the battle that would end the war in the spring of 1862.

Lincoln's Secretary of War Simon Cameron had been overwhelmed by the organizational needs of the growing army. After the initial press of volunteers, however, he had come up with a good plan to keep field regiments at full strength. In December 1861, he directed that once volunteer regiments came under federal jurisdiction, replacement troops would be forwarded by federal recruiters posted in the various states. Unfortunately, the ineffectual Cameron had too often proved a political embarrassment to the administration and his logical idea never received a chance to work. As a new year dawned, Lincoln replaced him with Edwin Stanton.[1]

Photo of the Stratton house from the 12th Rhode Island Infantry's regimental history. This brick dwelling was a wartime landmark. On the hilltop in the background is Brompton, the Marye house that was also a wartime structure.

This modern photo shows how the Stratton house has been carefully maintained and enlarged by a rear addition and a short extension to the side. Like most historic Fredericksburg homes, the house remains a private residence.

In January 1862, Stanton aggressively moved to end what he considered the abuses and waste of his predecessor's tenure, one aspect of which appeared to be the federal recruiting offices. In the spring of 1862, as McClellan finally began to move his Army of the Potomac to the Virginia Peninsula, Stanton thought there were enough troops for the task at hand and ordered the federal recruiting offices closed. To everyone's great surprise and consternation, the war did not conveniently end on the Peninsula.

In July 1862, Lincoln called for another 300,000 three-year volunteers. The state governors, who had watched the Federal authorities dismantle their recruiting stations, were not prepared to have to step in and raise troops again. Citizens were also less enthusiastic than the year before. During the military build-up of 1861-62, volunteer soldiers had too often succumbed to disease in camps and the U.S. Army appeared unable to figure out how to win the war. Three years loomed as an awful long time to endure miserable conditions and potential death.[2]

The crisis was real though, and the government needed men. As the summer progressed, Southern formations had secured Richmond from McClellan's mighty host and begun to bring the war closer to Washington D.C. A fight in Culpeper County, at Cedar Mountain, was followed by an advance into Fairfax County, where the Federals suffered a second defeat at Bull Run. Confederate forces then crossed the Potomac River into Maryland. As the crisis intensified without a sufficient number of volunteers coming forward, the Lincoln administration issued a call for 300,000 nine-month militia.

There were many three-year regiments recruited that summer and fall, but another 90,000 men responded to the call for a short-term obligation. Though another crisis would come about in the spring and summer of 1863, when those short-term enlistments expired, the immediate need for men was met reasonably well and the nine-month units served with honor. The 12th Rhode Island Infantry became a part of Brigadier General Samuel D. Sturgis's division in the Army of the Potomac's Ninth Corps. They spent their 1862 service in Virginia and fought at Fredericksburg in December of that year. They also experienced the Mud March, in January 1863, after which they departed Virginia when two Ninth Corps divisions were detached and transferred to Kentucky. They served the rest of their time in the west, until mustered out in July. The Rhode Island men did not serve long enough to experience victory, but they went west as veter-

Photo of Brompton, from the 12th Rhode Island Infantry's regimental history. This was the home of the Marye family during the war and is now owned and cared for by the University of Mary Washington.

This modern view shows how well the stone wall and grounds have been maintained.

ans, and their part in the battle of Fredericksburg is a prominent part of their regimental history.[3]

On December 13, 1862, the 12th Rhode Island Regiment, about 600 strong, was part of Brigadier General James Nagle's brigade, Sturgis's division. They were held in reserve on lower Caroline Street as Federal assaults slammed up against the Confederate position in a stone lined sunken road. Stray bullets smacked against buildings. Wounded men staggered past as those new to combat waited their turn to be fed into what appeared to be a horrible man-made storm. Around 2:30 p.m., Nagle advanced his brigade. As his units moved out from the relative protection of the town, they tried to guide on Frederick Street, but became disordered by the railway tracks that veered to the east. The inexperienced Rhode Island men lost cohesion as they tried to move forward, but regrouped in the shelter of a railway cut, in which there were not yet any tracks. Other regiments from the brigade also found that seemingly protected area, but Confederate artillery on Telegraph (Lee's) Hill had a clear field of fire down the constricted cut and the guns quickly found their range. The Federals scrambled up the embankment to escape the exploding shells, and stepped into Confederate small arms fire from the sunken road. As they formed on the open ground, some soldiers turned and fled, overwhelmed by the pandemonium of the heavy incoming fire and unnerved by the slippery blood soaked ground. The more stalwart soldiers took position among the wounded men and mangled corpses, about 100 yards from the Confederate line at the base of Willis Hill. They began to return fire, but their position was still within range of Telegraph (Lee's) Hill where Confederate infantry had taken position and the Federals found themselves in a cross-fire. The men of the 12th Rhode Island lay in the mud and the blood, firing their weapons, but no longer advancing. Other attacks to their left also failed. They were brought off after dark and their forlorn ordeal finally ended.[4]

When the Rhode Island veterans published their story, they included several photographs of the place where they had suffered their battle casualties. The historic photos shown below are from their regimental history. The modern views were taken by the editorial staff. The Fredericksburg battleground in front of Marye's Heights includes a preserved Sunken Road, with its stone walls, but the open terrain across which the Federal forces advanced has become a neighborhood. The railway cut is still evident, that deadly position now the scene of a hiking/biking trail. The Civil War era dwellings within range of the Sunken Road that were constructed in brick still survive and are occupied by Fredericksburg families. The wood frame structures did not last, except for a single modest house, which is maintained by the National Park Service. The preserved historic ground and the local neighborhood live comfortably adjacent to one another.

NOTES

1. Allan Nevins, *The War for the Union, Volume 1, The Improvised War 1861-1862* (New York: Charles Scribner's Sons, 1959), pp. 168-169.
2. *The War of the Rebellion: A Compilation of the Official Records of the Union and Confederate Armies* (Washington D.C.: Government Printing Office, 1890-1901), series 3, volume 5, p. 885.
3. *History of the Twelfth Regiment, Rhode Island Volunteers in the Civil War, 1862-1863* (Providence: Snow & Farnham, 1904).
4. Francis Augustin O"Reilly, *The Fredericksburg Campaign: Winter War on the Rappahannock* (Baton Rouge: Louisiana State University Press, 2003), pp. 343-347.

Index

A
Abernathy, Alice Heflin 10, 22, 23, 29n
Adams, J. William 92
Aler, George 51, 55, 75, 91

B
Bailey, D.W. 79
Ballou, Levi 11, 27n
Barksdale, William 98n
Barstow, W.H. 88-95
Bauman, F. 79-81, 85-89, 91-93, 97
Beadle, J.H. 31, 37
Beardsley, L.A. 57, 58, 60, 61, 64, 69, 72-74, 77, 85, 87, 89, 91, 94
Birdsall, Andrew J. 9, 10 photo, 19-21, 24, 26n, 28n
Birdsall, Julia A. 21
Blankman, M.A. 71, 74
Bowering, B.F. 94
Bowler, W.W. 88, 89, 91-96
Bradley, James H. 44-52, 54, 55, 60
Bragden, Charles E. 65, 71, 74
Branch, Thomas 66
Braxton, Carter M. 63, 65, 71, 77-79, 85
Braxton, E.M. 44-46, 48-51, 54, 96, 97
Brown, John 93
Burnside, Ambrose E. 12, 13

C
Cahill, Martin 45, 53
Canby, Edward Richard Sprigg 88, 89, 96, 101n
Carter 87
Casey, Peter Jaquith 23
Chaffee, Eustace 96
Chaffee, L.E. 79, 96
Chew, J.J. 55, 85

Chew, Robert S. 79, 81, 82, 85
Coakley, John 68
Coleman, Thomas S. 64, 69, 89, 90
Couse, Katherine 100n
Couse, Peter 56-58, 60, 61, 66, 67, 71-73, 77, 79-81, 86-89, 91, 92, 94-97, 100n
Creighton, John A. 90
Cronin, David E. 17
Cunningham, William H. 45-49, 51, 52, 54, 56, 58-62, 66-69, 71-73, 77

D

Davis, W. Wallace 61
Day, William 86
Dodge, Edward F. 105, 116n
Dolbar, D.S. 89-94
Dunn, P.B. 51, 88, 89, 91, 93-96
Dunn, T.B. 85

E

Ebert, August 103, 104, 106, 115, 116n
Edrington, Charles W. 45, 53, 66, 68, 80
Elder, John D. 59
Eldridge, M. 75
Ellis, D.C. 56-58, 60, 61, 64, 69, 71-75, 77, 82
Ellis, W.C. 81
Eve, George W. 56-61, 64, 67, 69-74, 77-82, 85-98

F

Farney, Thomas 107
Ficklen, George 96
Ficklen, James B. 44, 50, 74
Fielding, Amos 107-113, 115, 116n, 117n
Fitzhugh, St. George R. 44, 69, 77, 97
Folk, Samuel 96
Ford, James W. 52
Fortune, Albert 85
Frost, L.C. 56-58, 60, 61, 64, 66, 67, 69-72, 74-82, 84-89

G

Galland, Doctor 107, 109-111, 113, 115, 117n
Gordon, Stephen W. 113, 114
Gouldman, Mabel Wicks (Birdsall) 28n
Grant, Ulysses S. 31, 35, 37
Green, D. 44, 51, 55
Green, Duff 51, 55
Green, George S. 59
Green, James L. 50, 55
Greenough, G.G. 56, 58
Griffin, Thomas 64
Grove, Charles A. 85, 86
Gunn, G.S. 86

H

Hall, Joseph 82
Hancock, William G. 60, 61
Hancock, Winfield Scott 38n
Hansford, Monroe 34, 35, 39n
Harper, J. Newton 75
Hart, Robert 95
Hart, W. 59, 71, 89
Haslup, Edwin D. 88
Hayes, James 64
Hazard, Josiah 37 photo, 39n
Heflin, Florence (Birdsall) 28n
Heinichen, Edward L. 82, 92
Henderson, Mary G. 68
Hepler (Helper), A.G. 80
Hepler (Helper) C.G. 80
Herndon, Brodie S. 76, 96
Herndon, John M. 76, 93
Hicks, Hugh 93
Hicks, Wade H. 88
Hill, Thomas 97
Hirsh, Simon 50, 96, 97
Hoomes 78

Hoyer 67
Huffman, Landon J. 45, 51, 52, 59, 81, 94
Hunter, Charles E. 56-58, 60, 61, 64, 66, 68, 69, 71-73, 77, 79-82, 84-88, 95
Hurkamp, John G. 44, 46, 48, 49, 51, 53, 54, 56-62, 64, 67, 68, 71-78, 81
Hurt, Henry 10, 26n

I
Ingalls, J. Gary 24, 29n
Ingalls, Kent 9, 22, 24, 29n
Ingalls, Lucille Heflin 9, 23
Irvin, William 107-110, 112, 113, 115, 116n, 117n

J
Jackson, W.H. 34, 38n
Jaquith, Abigail (Abbie) 18
Jaquith, Franklin 18, 20
Jaquith, Franklin Jr. 18
Jaquith, Joseph 19
Jaquith, Lucy 18
Jaquith, Mary 18
Jefferies, William J. 49, 56-58, 60, 61, 64, 66, 67, 69, 71-74, 77, 79-81, 85-98
Jennings, Washington 80, 86
Johnson (Colonel) 53
Johnson, Andrew 99n, 100n
Jones, William J. 59, 66

K
Kelley (Major) 90
Kelly, J.H. 78
King, William H. 60
Knox, Thomas F. 46, 48, 49, 51, 52, 78
Kruger, Louis 103-107, 116n

L

Lamb, H.H. 96
Landram, Edward L. 31, 38n
Langer, William 79
Larkin, John B. 53
Lee, Robert E. 37
Lincoln, Abraham 11, 13, 43, 100n, 119
Little, William A. 44-46, 48, 49, 52-54, 56-61, 64-67, 72-75, 77
Lordley, Thomas E. 59
Lordly, Joseph E. 59
Ludwig 67
Lynch, James 107-113, 116n, 117n

M

Mallam, Charles E. 56-58, 60, 61, 64, 66-74, 77, 78, 80, 81, 83-88, 100n
Mannix, John 59
Manuel, Thomas 77, 78
Markey, L.P. 58, 59, 66, 98
Martin, Mary Anne 9
Marye, John L. 53, 98
Mason, Patricia 10, 11, 27n
Mazeen, James 45, 51, 73
McClain 94
McClellan, George B. 37, 119
McGuire, James 44-46, 50-53, 55, 98
Miller, Catherine 114
Miller, Charles 87-89, 91, 92, 94-98, 103-107, 110-112, 114, 115n, 116n
Miller, George 103-106, 112-115
Miller, George Jr. 114
Miller, Henrietta 114
Miller, Henry 79-81, 85-89, 92, 93, 95-97
Miller, Sophia 114
Minor, Betty 77
Montgomery, Morris 59, 79
Moon, Bessie Loreen (Birdsall) 28n
Moon, William J. 64
Morrison, William C. 56, 57, 60, 61, 64, 66, 73, 74, 77, 80, 81, 85-87, 96

Morton, Alfred 88, 90
Murray 85
Myers, G.A. 67

N
Nagle, James 123
Nye, William E. 88-98

O
Owens (Mrs.) 35

P
Payne, Elzay 69
Peabody, George 99n
Peirce, Albinia (Allie) Jaquith 10, 11 photo, 12, 18-20, 23, 26n, 27n, 28n
Peirce, Charles Jerome 11
Peirce, Jerome 8 photo, 9-20, 22-25, 26n, 27n, 28n
Peirce, Joseph 11
Peirce, Lucy Sherwin cover photo, 10, 11, 19, 20, 26n, 28n
Peirce, Martha Sherwin 11
Perry, George Washington 34, 38n
Peyton, George H. 64
Phillips, A.K. 45
Pierpont, Francis H. 101n

Q
Quinn, Sylvanus J. 91, 101n

R
Rawlett, G.A. 51
Reed 91
Richardson, Samuel P. 61, 91, 92
Roberts, F.W. 53
Rowe, Absalom P. 44-50, 54-57, 59, 61, 66, 67, 69, 72-74, 78
Russell, Alonzo H. 107, 110

S

Sanford, Joseph 17
Savage, Thomas L. 59
Schofield, John M. 40 photo, 53, 56, 58-60, 64, 65, 99n
Scott, William S. 50
Sears, Barnas 49, 99n
Sears, Hector 53, 99n
Sedgwick, John 34, 35, 37, 39n
Sener, J.B. 45
Sener, James W. 44-52, 54, 55, 60, 73
Sherman, William T. 17, 116n
Slaughter, Montgomery 44-46, 48, 49, 51, 52, 55-58
Smith, Augusta (Birdsall) 28n
Smith, J.B. 16
Smith, J.F. 45
Smith, William C. 59
Staiars, Robert 67
Stanton, Edwin 99n, 119, 121
Straight, C.L. 79, 91
Straight, William E. 79-81, 83, 87-97
Stringfellow, P. Laurence 89, 90
Sturgis, Samuel D. 121, 123
Sullivan, Thomas 60

T

Tackett, John E. 75
Taliaferro, E.H. 89, 91
Taylor, Robert A. 90
Thompson, Duncan, Jr. 96-98
Timberlake, George H. 53
Timberlake, John S.G. 68
Toombs 88
Trigg, Catherine 34

U

Underhill, A.C. 79

131

W

Waite 51, 73
Walker, Robert 45
Wallace, C. Wistar 74, 94, 96
Way, William 80
Wellford, B.R. 52
Wellford, C.C. 92, 99n
Wells, Henry H. 101n
Wheeler, Charles H. 58, 59
White, William 60
Williams, John 55
Wilson, John 107-113, 115, 116n, 117n
Woodward, Philip G. 13, 16, 27n
Wright, Washington 93
Wroten, George W. 44, 46, 48-52

Y

Young, John James 44, 46-48, 51